ONE MAN IN HIS TIME

ONE MAN
IN HIS TIME
An Autobiography

by
ALICK WEST

London
GEORGE ALLEN & UNWIN LTD
RUSKIN HOUSE, MUSEUM STREET

PRINTED IN GREAT BRITAIN
in 11 on 12 point Times Roman
BY BLACKFRIARS PRESS LTD
LEICESTER

For Elizabeth

CHAPTER I

My mother must have been ill for a long time; for I remember, as if it were something we did every day, helping my brothers to cut off from her bread the crust which irritated her throat – or I believe I remember it. I remember being taken to her room; and her head slowly turned towards me on the pillow.

I remember the day she died. My two brothers and I – they were both older than me – were playing with our bricks on the nursery floor when our father came in, sat down on the end of a couch and called us over to him. When we had gathered round him, he said, 'Mother's gone to stay with Jesus'. I didn't understand. Then I saw my brothers begin to cry and my father bow his head and cover his face with his hands. As if – I thus described it to myself in memory – I had a little man inside me watching me, I wondered whether I also would cry.

But though from the age of five I had no mother, I was part of a family. Nobody of that family now remains except my sister, Constance, and sometimes I think how lonely I should be if she were to die. So I am more aware that a family has been around me all my life.

I know little of my father's life, and now all his experience is gone. Son of a nonconformist clergyman from Manchester, he had wanted to be a doctor, but his mother had forbade it. He had been apprenticed in his early teens – he was born in 1859 – to the engineering firm of Beyer and Peacock, and to be in time for work he had to get up at five o'clock. As no alarm could waken him, he fixed up a contrivance by which the clock dropped a cushion on his head. When he got back in the evening, he was so tired that he would fall asleep while he was saying his prayers, so he made it a rule to say them before he had his supper. Sometime in his early twenties he gave up engineering to become a missionary, and after studying at a theological college in New Zealand he went to India. He told us that the sailing ship on which he made the voyage to New Zealand had almost foundered in a storm, and the captain had come down and said, 'There's not much hope now'; and 'foundered' became for me a word of doom. On his return

7

to England he went into engineering again, and in 1890 married my mother, daughter of a well-known Baptist minister in Manchester. From the way my father spoke about her, though he said very little, I am sure that they were and remained deeply in love. Though he ceased to be a missionary, he remained strongly religious and uncompromising in his moral standards; he once told me that he had given up the small engineering business he had taken over because he found that he had to tell lies. He moved with his family into a village in Warwickshire, and occupied himself with reading, writing stories which were never published, studying by correspondence for a degree at London University which he never took, and building an organ, on which he used to play hymn tunes and simple voluntaries. After my mother's death we moved to Highgate, into one of the new red-brick houses in Talbot Road with protuberant bow-windows and stained-glass in the front door, and a wooden-fenced back-garden.

My father's unmarried sister came to live with us, and his mother, whom we called Granny. She wore a white lace cap, and on each side of her face hung long hollow curls. She always wore a black silk dress and a purple petticoat, in the pocket of which she kept jujubes and soft tissue paper. The house was run by a housekeeper, and two servants were kept.

My father went every day by train to work for the Charity Organisation Society in the East End, for which he was paid £2 a week. Such, at least, was the figure which fixed itself in my head; and so I thought that we lived on £104 a year. With my pocket-money of a penny a week I bought Christmas and birthday presents and a 'ha'porth of humbugs'. Once on my father's birthday I gave him flowers from my patch in the garden, among them a long-spurred yellow columbine I was very fond of, and said that I had no money to give him anything else. He said, 'I only want your love'; and I felt dishonest, for I had had twopence.

In my conscious world, money had, I think, neither more nor less importance than such memories. What was the actual income of my father and his mother, I don't know, but I should guess it must have been near £1,000, derived from prudent investments. When the boys at school asked me what my father was, I replied, 'He's a gentleman at large'.

8

I felt secure because I knew what I had to do. Every day at the same time I had to set out for school – first to Miss Legg's, then to Highgate Junior School; and I can't remember being late. When I came home, I had to go to the Tradesmen's side door, where Violet, the housemaid, let me in. I had to hang up my things and wash my hands. Meals were always punctual. In the dining-room, where the oil portraits of three or four generations followed me with their eyes, I had my place. Before we sat down, grace was said by my father, or by Granny when he was not there. After we had been given permission to leave the table, my brothers and I could go and play; but in the evening we had to do our homework. I went to bed at bedtime; and when I had undressed, I knelt and said my prayers.

At the time when my father could be expected back from the East End, my brothers and I would sometimes go down to the station to meet the trains, and we could recognize his hand as it stretched down from the carriage window to turn the handle. If he had come back without our meeting him, we would ask each other, 'What sort of mood is he in?' If the report was that he was 'in a wax', with trepidation we entered his study to do our homework. Leaning back in his chair, with his feet on a bureau, he smoked and read books on religion. We worked silently, with an occasional furtive glance at each other or an encouraging grin. From time to time our father came and looked over our shoulder at our exercises and sums. If we had done them wrong and he was 'in a bait', our wits deserted us. The bureau was opened, the strap taken out, and the helpless one was whipped round the calves. He blundered more, and was sent to bed.

When he was not in a bait, he would rumple our hair and lay his firm hand on our shoulders, and I would catch the loved smell from his brown Norfolk jacket. He would read to us from Grimm's *Fairy Tales, The Pilgrim's Progress,* or *Oliver Twist.*

When I was about nine, my brothers were sent away to boarding school. If in the evening my father had not come back from the East End in time to say goodnight to me, I felt alone and miserable. So on the way home from school I would tread on certain cracks in the pavement to make it certain that he would be back. If he hadn't come, I lay in bed listening to the trains and then for my father's step. Sometimes I grew afraid of the darkness in the room, and through the crevice under a door in the wall giving into a boxroom I imagined I saw sparks as if there were a fire raging. I used to have nightmares of the house on fire, until I dreamt that only one half of the house was burning and I was in the other half, watching; after that, the dream never returned. Then I became afraid of the world outside our house, as if my father were no longer anywhere in it. Even when I was not afraid, I listened as if anything might happen. Once I heard a voice so beautiful that I thought it must come from heaven; I went to the window, and saw a man beneath a lamp-post playing the violin. Another time I looked out and saw the sky full of stars, and drew back my head, terrified. When I had been waiting for my father to come and at last I heard his steps, then I was happy. If he went to his study, I called 'Father, Father'; then he came in and spoke to me lovingly, and brought me a glass of cold water from the filter in the cellar. But the next night that he was out late the fear returned that he might have died. Not even his presence could always banish the thought of his death. When round the piano on Sunday evenings the hymns were sung, I could not command my voice to sing with him 'Soon will you and I be lying, Each within his narrow bed'.

Just as I felt for my father both love and fear, so also I loved God and dreaded His anger. 'Two women shall be grinding the corn; one shall be taken, the other left.' Would I be taken or my sister? 'Constance shall be taken, Alick shall be left', 'Alick shall be taken, Constance shall be left' – which sounded more likely? One evening I remembered I had told a lie, and in terror that I should be sent to hell I knelt down on the floor where I was doing my homework, and prayed to be forgiven. I had hardly got up from my knees when my father came in and brought me a present – a red leather pocket-book. Yet not long afterwards I lost it; and when at school one of the masters came round the class asking if anybody had lost a red pocket-book, I didn't stand up.

Though the family was a unity, there was also division. My brothers and I helped each other against our father, but we were also rivals. When we were on our walks in the open country round Finchley and Totteridge and stopped to pump ship in the hedge, we would say 'Bags I next Father'; and if I had said it first, I would take his hand when we started walking again. My eldest brother Graeme, and I used to join together for no reason against Cecil (I remember from the time before my mother's death that among our Noah's Ark animals there was a cow with a broken leg which Graeme and I used to call 'Cecil'). Sometimes they turned against me because I was the youngest, and I was sorry for myself, having all the disadvantages of the youngest brother and none of the advantages of Constance, by four years the youngest child. But I also remember how my brothers and I were once looking out of our bedroom window when I was about seven or eight, and I put my arms round their shoulders and said 'I love you'.

The household was divided into family and servants, to whom the housekeeper and the nurse didn't quite belong; and we were aware of the division. We liked the servants; and in the kitchen we felt free. We enjoyed it when Violet, the housemaid, came into the nursery and sang *Bill Bailey*. When the housekeeper, finding her in the nursery, jerked with her thumb over her shoulder, 'Now then, Vi'let, out of my sitting-room!', we were on Violet's side. But I did not pray for the servants; and when they came to family prayers before breakfast, they had to sit in the corner by the door.

And the house had two entrances. Like the tradesmen and the servants, I had to use the side-entrance; but I knew that this was because I was a child, and that one day I should go in and out at the front door, as I already did with my father.

He was the authority who maintained the division and the difference; and I knew that the servants' obedience to him was different from ours. He was justice as well as authority. One Sunday evening my nurse was seeing me to bed, and she was quietly crying. When my father came in to say goodnight to me, he asked her what was the matter. She said that the housekeeper had grumbled at her for wanting to go to chapel when the servants were out and leaving her to look after everything, so she had stayed in. My father immediately left the room. After some minutes he came back. Using words which I had never heard before, and which sounded with tremendous power, he said that he had given the housekeeper his 'strict injunctions'.

11

In the world outside was the division between rich and poor. We were not very rich, I thought; but there was the same distance between us and the poor as between us and the servants; and again my father embodied this order. He went to the East End to help the poor if they were deserving; but he had no need of anyone to help him.

Yet there was a power standing even higher than he. One morning, as the housekeeper placed the tea-tray on the breakfast table and carefully straightened it, she said to my father, 'The worst has hapened, sir'. 'The Queen?' asked my father. She nodded, and the Venetian blinds were let down. The throne stood above us all. So did the law. One day my father took me down a turning where a notice said 'Private Road'. I said, 'It says Private Road'. My father laughed, but I was still afraid.

Privacy was inviolable. My father said that I must never look in at other people's windows; Granny told us not to touch our own carefully looped curtains lest passers-by or the people on the opposite side of the street should see us looking out. But the row of slummy cottages, with their doors always open, which I passed on my way to school – these were not private. In the back-garden we could play Robinson Crusoe and Red Indians, and make a noise; but between us and the world before the front windows there was a separating silence. When somebody was ill in a neighbouring house, straw was put down in the roadway to muffle the sound of the horses' hoofs; and it was as if all the sights and sounds from without were deadened by the curtain of privacy that shut us off from our neighbours.

Certainly there is a different quality in the memories of the farm where my brothers and sister and I went with our nurse, Miss Wise, every summer holiday. It was in the hamlet of Yarningale, in Warwickshire, and nearby was a common with a little hill from which you could see as far as the Wrekin. The farm must have been about fifty acres, and a canal ran through the lower fields. It was farmed by Joe Smith, a vigorous red-haired man of about thirty, who liked to rub his ginger stubble against our cheeks until we screamed; and his two sisters ran the house and looked after the hens and the dairy. The red-brick timbered house was friendly, with a flagged porch, on which I pounded grains of corn to make flour and bake a small

12

loaf. Here there was no division and no separating privacy. The door usually stood open, and we all ate together. My brothers and I helped to find the hens' eggs; we chopped up nettles and mixed them with meal for the turkeys. We helped to bring in the harvest, and chased the rabbits as they dashed out of the dwindling square of standing corn. We knew all the cows by name and were allowed to try our hand at milking. We could tell by the sound when the butter was forming in the churn. We played on the common with the boys from the cottages. We formed a band, 'The Yarningale Pirates', I being the powder-monkey; we wrote out the laws on a large piece of white cardboard, signed our names in our blood, and at the end of the holidays buried the charter in the bed of a stream. I remember also that I ate a toadstool, taking a bite from a pear to hide the taste, because I wanted to die and see heaven. But I used to cry bitterly when we had to go back to the house in Talbot Road.

In 1905, when I was ten, my father married again. He was now forty-six, and our stepmother was five years younger. He had met her in the East End, where she had been working in a settlement.

How he prepared us for her coming, I don't remember; but for some reason we believed him to have said to her that if she would not marry him he would live in one room in the East End on sixpence a week. I recall that we were taken to see two new aunts: the moustached and creaking widow of an Indian Army chaplain, and her tremulous spinster sister. At the next visit, our stepmother made her entry. Tactfully, she only shook hands with us. To me she said, 'And this is Alick, of whom I have heard so much'; and I noticed the grammatical correctness. When she came home after the wedding, which was in Ireland, I was having my milk and cream crackers before going to bed. We sat facing each other across the corner of the table. I knew she didn't know what to say, so I went on eating. At last she said, 'Foraging in the biscuit box?'

Not long afterwards I brought home a bunch of wild flowers and took them to her in the drawing-room, where I could hear her singing an Irish song and accompanying herself on the piano. She went on playing; and in a slow intoning voice she said, 'Thank you, Darling. They're lovely.' 'Why do you speak

13

in that funny voice?' I asked. 'Because,' she answered, 'of the music.' But unwillingly I liked it when, stroking the back of my head, in rather the same kind of voice she said, 'My moley'.

During the same time, I was saying to my brothers, as if I were aggrieved, that she didn't like me. I also found I could start crying whenever I wanted, and I did so, until Graeme, who had a sense of responsibility towards us all and saw that the habit was doing me harm, said that if I didn't stop he would tell Father. I did stop; and I didn't say any more that M'amie, as she asked us to call her, didn't like me.

But I was jealous. She would send me out of the room, saying, 'This is my time with Father'. Or, as if she were being very kind, she would say, 'Now you can go and put the cuff-links in Father's shirt and keep him company while he dresses for dinner'—for that was what he now had to do.

Because my father was a gentleman, he should dress for dinner, and I must begin learning to be a gentleman and put the links in his shirt. To Granny she said sharply that it was 'unladylike' to lick the marmalade off her knife. We also now heard the word 'cultured'. When my grandmother spoke of 'the Book', she meant the Bible, and we knew it was different from all other books: *Pilgrim's Progress* was a 'good book', and so was Foxe's *Book of Martyrs*, and we knew what that meant also; all other books, whether they were Grimm's *Fairy Tales* or *Oliver Twist*, were story books. But now we heard of books that 'cultured people' read, and a complete set of Thackeray appeared.

We no longer went to Yarningale farm for our holidays, but to France. In the first winter after their marriage my father took my stepmother to Egypt for her bronchitis; and I remember how Constance and I were having tea when their ship was in the Mediterranean, and I balanced my spoon on the rim of my cup and made the bowl swing to and fro on the tea, saying that it was 'The City of Corinth', and then pushed the spoon so that the bowl filled with tea and sank, and Constance cried out.

We moved after a year or two from the red brick and privet hedges of Talbot Road to the white-painted early Regency Holly Terrace on West Hill overlooking the great trees on the Baroness Burdett-Coutts estate. A veranda ran the length of the house, and in between its railings and around the supports of the roof and over into the verandas of our neighbours grew a magnificent wistaria, which scented all the lofty rooms.

I went on from Highgate junior school to the upper school; Cecil joined Graeme at Blundell's. While I was still a boy, I asked my father why he had not sent me to a boarding school. He replied in the enigmatic tone which his voice sometimes had, 'Because of what Bishop Creighton said'; and he would say no more.

Then I was baptized. I had not been baptized before because my father believed, like the Anabaptists, that it should wait until I knew what I was doing; but my stepmother, who belonged to the Church of Ireland, perhaps persuaded him otherwise. I was sent to a confirmation class taken by a High Church clergyman in a cassock, and I thought that I too was to be confirmed. Then I discovered that in a few days' time I was to be merely baptized. It was to be done in the late afternoon. We had been having tea in the garden, and rather moodily I was standing around by myself when my stepmother came over to me and said, 'Are you thinking of the promises you are going to make?' I wasn't, and I resented the question. The ceremony didn't move me; on the rim of the font was a clean handkerchief folded as if it had just come from the laundry, and the water was dabbed off my forehead with it.

The religious feeling in the family lost its intensity. My father once said to me when I was grown up that after my mother's death 'the heavens were as brass above me', and that he had almost lost his faith in God. That he did not lose it, was not because he became accustomed or reconciled to her having died, but rather, I think, because his sense of loss became inseparable from the thought of God, so that during the years of our childhood he was constantly thinking of God. The circumstances of his own life intensified his dissenters' tradition that religion is in a man's own personal being, not in ritual. It was so much a part of his own being that for me, whether I loved or feared him, he was a man who believed in God; and because he believed, so did I. When he laid his hand on my forehead as I lay in bed and said, 'God bless you, dear lad,' for both of us God was living and had the power and love to bless. When my brothers were away at school, he used to take

15

me with him on Sundays to Baptist and Unitarian chapels in Hampstead, and as we walked home across Parliament Fields he used to talk to me about the sermons and the love of God, and he once said that he was glad that I could understand. After the coming of my stepmother, we went only to the Church of England, and he and I talked no more together about religion.

We were still very close to each other. Until I was about thirteen or fourteen, he still came upstairs with me to the bedroom at the top of the house and saw me into bed. He smoked his pipe while I did pull-ups and belly-presses because I was so small for my age and wanted to become strong, and he waited patiently while every night for some months, when I was about twelve, I went through a peculiar performance.

Sitting up in bed, I pretended to pull at a bell. My ring being answered, I crawled under the clothes to the bottom of the bed. In the darkness I enacted excited greetings from my three imaginary children, George, Arthur and Birt (the last two names were my father's). After they had recited the day's exploits, I crawled out and my father gave me a piece of chocolate. When he had put out the gas and was leaving the room, I called out in a squeaky voice, 'Goodnight, grandfather'; and he responded in a gruff bass, 'Goodnight, Birt'. Only once did he say in a resigned voice, 'You're a rum lad'.

But after his marriage to my stepmother, she, rather than my father, became the centre of the family. Granny, who had lost her memory, was put into a home, and her place was taken by 'Grandm'amie', as we were told to call her. She also wore a white cap, but no curls; and she would never have lifted her dress to give us jujubes from her petticoat pocket. Nor would she have forbidden us, as Granny forbade us, to use the word 'luck', since all things took place by the will of God. The feeling of the old family still seemed to be in my father, breaking out in sudden violent contradictions of my stepmother's judgments and in the fierce scorn with which he repeated his favourite saying, 'They say. What say they? Let them say.' But the tone of the family changed as my stepmother turned our thoughts away from ourselves to the world outside. When my brothers were home for the holidays, she encouraged us in our arguments about the rival merits of our schools. I was proud that Highgate

School was fifty years the older and had been founded, not like Blundell's by a draper, but by a knight, Sir Roger Cholmeley. Because I argued well, my stepmother said I should become a barrister or go into Parliament.

As I believed in the duty of loyalty to my school, so I believed in the duty of loyalty to my country. When I was doing my homework alone in the room at the top of the house and on summer evenings heard from Parliament Fields the distant sound of a band playing 'God Save the King', I got up and stood to attention. When I was about fifteen, we were all strolling one evening through the Hampshire village where we were spending the summer holidays (we had stayed in England because Granny was slowly dying), and we stopped on the edge of a crowd round an open-air meeting in the market-place. The speaker was attacking the House of Lords. After we had listened for a little while, I sang out in my treble voice 'God Save the House of Lords'. My stepmother said, 'Well done, Alick!'

But as we moved off, I heard the speaker saying, 'Now that our aristocratic friends have left . . . 'I felt uneasy, as if I had done something I should be ashamed of, even though it pleased my stepmother. About the same time she gave me for my birthday a school story about Harrow by H. A. Vachell, *The Hill.* I liked to think that our school also stood on its hill; and I identified myself with the hero, John Verney, and wished that I was called by my first name, John, instead of Alick. But one of the masters said to him, 'You pride yourself on being straight, but to me you are as straight as a question mark'; and the words stuck in my mind.

Then when I was fifteen, I was reading again *The Fifth Form at St Dominic's,* in which one of the boys steals a paper containing the questions for a scholarship examination. Suddenly I remembered that in the examination when I had won a foundation scholarship that paid my school fees, I had cribbed. I had been uncertain whether to give the future infinitive of a Latin verb in the form *facturus esse* or *facturum esse,* and had looked to see what the boy next to me had written; he had put *facturum esse,* so I did the same. Till this moment I had forgotten. I wished I had never picked up the book that made me remember. What ought I to do? I must tell my father; then

he could write to the headmaster. For about three months the
burden lay on my conscience. I kept remembering the line
in *Hamlet:* 'Can one be pardoned and retain the offence?' Again
and again I was on the brink of speaking. When we were on our
holidays in France, cycling along the straight roads, and my
father was riding alone a little way ahead of me (I can see the
label bearing the French railway registration number '17' stuck
askew on the back mudguard), I thought I would overtake him
and tell him, 'Father, I cribbed in the scholarship examination'.
In a boys' story by R. M. Ballantyne I read words that gave
me no rest: 'Meditation, unless it results in action, is worse than
useless; for it only deepens condemnation'. At last, one Sunday
morning, before going to school chapel, I went down to his
study and said to him, 'Father, I've got something terrible to
tell you'. After I had told him, we sat down on the sofa and
he held me close and said, 'You have made me very happy,
because you have shown you have a high sense of honour'. I
felt relief that the load was off my mind, but I also felt emptied.
As my father continued to hold me to him, I felt a button pressing against my cheekbone. My father then said that my action
had not affected the results of the examination and that I could
keep my scholarship; and I was disappointed that nothing more
was to happen. Nevertheless, on that Sunday evening, when I
said goodnight to my father in the drawing-room, while my stepmother read her book, ignorant of what had happened between
us, I felt there was renewed love.

Then I started remembering lies I had told, and on four or
five mornings when my father came to call me I confessed them
to him. On my way to the bathroom I met my stepmother on
the landing and confessed a lie to her. But with each confession
I felt less lightening of heart and became aware that my father
didn't know what to say. So I stopped confessing.

Towards the end of the same year I was to be confirmed.
It was by my own wish, and my self-examination before the
confirmation classes took the place of the confessions I could
no longer make to my father. But the outward circumstances
disappointed me. From translating Livy or Homer I would
be summoned to the class-room of the clergyman in charge of
the confirmation candidates; standing beside his desk, I would
repeat in a low voice the week's portion of the catechism,

resenting that the clergyman was dividing his attention between me and his class. The private talk with the headmaster was incomprehensible. Ginger-haired, florid and afflicted with carbuncles, he said that he supposed I knew what was meant by 'the desires of the flesh'. Deciding that it must mean wanting to eat and drink, I answered 'Yes'. 'When you are tempted by these desires,' he said 'think of your sister.' Baffled, I said nothing. At the ceremony, I didn't like the foxy face of the Bishop nor the cold feel of his hands on my head. In the evening, when I was doing my homework upstairs, my stepmother came in. 'The pure flower of a blameless life,' she said, and placed on the table a vase with a spray of the same white lilies as in the picture of the Annunciation beside her bed; and I couldn't understand why she should have chosen these flowers.

The following Sunday I went for the first time to Holy Communion. I tried to feel that Christ was entering my soul, and myself tried to be my soul; but a separation remained. One evening in the following year, I had been saying my prayers at my bedside, trying to judge the intensity with which I said them; and then as I got into bed and pulled up the clothes, I said out loud, 'God is subjective'.

When I was seventeen, one Sunday evening I was preparing the Scripture lesson in the study, where my father was reading. I happened to come on the passage telling how Absalom fell in love with his sister, and pretending to be sick asked her to bring food to his bed, and lay with her. In my body, while my unknowing father went on reading, I discovered from the mounting erection the power of sexual desire.

At night, when I went to bed, I used to stand at my bedroom window and watch the lovers from Parliament Fields slowly going up West Hill, their arms twined round each other. Then I prayed to be given strength to be pure, but I went to Holy Communion only half desiring it and not much disturbed by the thought that I was eating and drinking to my own damnation.

CHAPTER II

I left school at the end of 1913. My brothers were already at the university: Cecil was at Trinity College, Dublin, where he was studying medicine, and Graeme had won a scholarship to Balliol in 1911. I also was to go up to Balliol in the autumn of 1914. I would read Greats, and then sit the examination for the Home Civil Service. I accepted without enthusiasm this future; but I was glad when my father said that I should first go to Germany. I was to be boarded with a schoolmaster, Herr Dr Oelgarte, in a village on the Baltic coast north of Stettin, and I was to leave after Christmas.

In the mornings I worked at German with Frau Oelgarte, and in the afternoon during the first weeks I went skating on the Bodden, as it was called, a great stretch of frozen water separated from the Baltic Sea by a thin tongue of land. As I came on the ice, I heard the village boys and girls saying 'Der Engländer' and laughing as I tried frantically to keep my balance. When I was more sure of myself, I skated far out over the black ice and then looked back at the straggle of skaters stretching out from the village, which in the late afternoon became silhouetted against the sky. As the twilight thickened over the expanse of ice, I heard the slow rhythmic ringing of iron and out of the misty gloom appeared the figure of a fisherman, lunging and swaying steadily from side to side as he drove himself onwards with a long pole.

In the evenings, I played erratic chess with Herr Oelgarte's orphaned nephew, Otto, a boy of about fourteen: and while Frau Oelgarte, whose pregnancy I was slow to realize, sewed clothes for the baby, her husband would spread out upon the sitting-room table the genealogical tree of the Oelgartes, whose remote connection with the family of Goethe he was now exploring. As he pored over the papers he sniffed continuously; admonished by his wife – 'Friedrich, wo ist dein Taschentuch?' – he tugged out a handkerchief and blew into it like an irritated baby. I was amused, and in the domestic atmosphere I was at ease.

Free now from family control, I lay in bed in the morning till

Frau Oelgarte knocked gently and said with mild reproach, 'Herr West, es ist neun Uhr'. At night I no longer said my prayers. On Sundays I went with the Oelgarte family to the red-brick Lutheran church, around whose lofty spire the ravens circled. I entered it with less awe than I would a church at home. But I recognized the Lord's Prayer, spoken by the whole congregation with a noise like the sea, while the accompanying music of the organ, soaring as if there were no roof above us but infinite space, moved me with unaccountable sadness and excitement.

Frau Oelgarte told me that, as a guest from another country, I must call upon the mayor, the vicar, the doctor, the headmaster of the school and the other members of the staff. I wrote out visiting cards with my name, and 'London' in one corner and 'Cammin' in the other as if, I thought, I were a firm with two branches; presented them, and conversed in halting German. With the Oelgartes I was invited to 'pleasant evenings', at which the wives sat on one side of the room and sewed and drank tea, and the men sat on the other and smoked and drank beer, and I was sent back and forth between them. How did I like Germany? I was asked; and would there be a war? I said that I liked Germany, and that there would be no war. Then we all sang the German song, *Gaudeamus igitur*.

To celebrate my nineteenth birthday Frau Oelgarte gave a party for about a dozen boys and girls. We wore German peasants' dress and danced on a small top landing, and for the first time I had wine and got a little drunk. Next day Otto teased me into the belief, which Frau Oelgarte maternally encouraged, that I had fallen in love with Lotte, the daughter of the postmaster. I had also become friendly with the doctor's son, Willi, who similarly believed himself in love; and on fine afternoons – the winter was now over – we rowed out into the bay, I with the pipe Lotte had given me for my birthday, and he with his beribboned guitar, and sang German folksongs. I wrote a poem.

Really I was not in love with Lotte, and I knew that I was acting up to what others had suggested. I didn't much want to kiss her, and was also checked by the thought that a kiss would be a promise to marry. I had no such thought when on one of my solitary walks along the cobbled roads that ran through the

21

flat land I saw ahead of me a girl whose dress showed that she was poor. I overtook her, and she turned her head and looked at me. I walked near her for a few moments, and then put my arm round her waist, and said, 'You are beautiful'. 'What kind of a girl do you take me for?' she said, and walked on.

When on my walks I smoked Lotte's pipe and sang Willi's songs, I was complacently happy. I was a young Englishman in Germany, and I would tell traveller's tales. But when I walked the roads hoping to find again the girl I had half embraced, I wasn't playing a part. I sat down, tired, on the verge of the road. Nobody passed, except occasionally a farmer walking by the head of the nodding horse between the shafts of a creaking waggon. The earth seemed empty; and sometimes I heard a throbbing pulsation as if far away a deep string were being slowly plucked.

I went for walks also with Herr Oelgarte; and as my German improved we discussed politics. We talked of the kinship between our two nations and regretted that England was allied with France instead of with Germany against Russia, and I wrote to my father about these talks.

I had come to Germany for three months, which had seemed a long time; and when they were over, there would still be six months before I should have to go up to Oxford. But soon it was April, and I went to Paris for two months. On my way through Berlin I met Lotte and took her to the theatre. As we drove back in a cab to the hotel where she was staying with her parents, I said, to break a long silence, 'He goes quick'; and as I spoke, I knew what she would answer, and felt cross with her and myself when she said it: 'Are you glad?'

On the way to Paris I went on a walking tour through the Black Forest. I was excited because for the first time I was doing something I had planned; and I greatly enjoyed the walking and the springtime and seeing the kingcups on the hillside pastures marking the course of invisible streams when I came out of the dark forests.

In Paris I was to stay in the house of a 'cellist who played in one of the leading orchestras. I thought I was to be, as in the Oelgarte household, the only other person in the family; but there were other boarders – an Englishman and two Swedish girls, a little older in years and a great deal older in manner than I, who might easily have passed for fifteen or sixteen. I felt that they had been looking forward to the arrival of another man to make up their quartet; but when they were giggling and throwing cushions, I sat still. I sang my German songs in my room, and I sent Lotte a photograph of myself, signed in small writing on the darkest part 'Immer Dein Alick'.

But some evenings I suddenly became gay and excited, said whatever came into my head, made them all laugh, and put my arms round the girls' waists. Once they sent me away, and through the thin wall of my bedroom I heard the pretty and friendly girl saying, 'Il est très gentil, mais il ne comprend absolument rien.'

After working in the mornings I often went to Notre Dame and the Louvre. On our holidays in France we had always visited churches and galleries. I tried hard to respond as I believed I ought to, and to know what I felt. I enjoyed the German and Italian primitives, the landscapes seen through a window, and flowering bushes against a sky like the evening; and I liked to come back to Ghirlandaio's picture of an old man with a kindly face and white stubble on his chin and a boy in a red hat looking up at him trustingly. I wanted to be able to say what is art. As I stood looking at a picture, I felt a tension between the stillness of the picture and time, which was like the tension when I heard the deep string throbbing in the distance. So I thought that perhaps I was an artist. In Notre Dame I was glad when I felt a moment of awe, and afterwards I wrote a sonnet.

When I came out of churches and museums, with undefined expectancy I turned off into side-streets on the Left Bank, where there was a smell of drains, and cabbage leaves in the gutter, and the windows were shuttered. I stopped for a moment outside a shop that showed photographs of naked women. Yet I hardly looked at girls; and although I knew the Greek and Latin words for prostitute and all those marked in the lexicons 'sensu obscoeno', consciously I never saw a prostitute. Outside a small café I sat down at an iron table and watched. I only drank one cup of coffee. Obedient to my father, I was careful of money. Perhaps once a week I bought four Gauloise cigarettes for ten centimes. Even so, I saw apprehensively my gold

23

twenty franc pieces becoming fewer. But I never imagined myself without money, just as I could not imagine myself without family and home.

I returned to Germany in July and stayed at Halle with my friend Willi, who was a student there. At the end of the month my stepmother and Constance were to join me for the summer holidays, and my father and Graeme and Cecil were to come later. There was already talk of war, but Willi and I went our long walks and sang our German folk songs and talked of Lotte, and he made sketches of old castles and I asked him why he was so fond of ruins. But the news became worse, and Willi went home. Outside the newspaper offices groups stood reading the latest telegrams. I heard them accuse England of treachery, and thought I should defend my country.

My stepmother and Constance came, and we met again in Gotha. We were told that if war was declared we should be able to return home after mobilization, so we did not take the last train to Holland. We watched the German soldiers, wreathed with flowers and singing 'In der Heimat, in der Heimat', march to the station through the cheering crowds, and to my surprise my stepmother said, 'At home we don't know what patriotism is'.

In the middle of August we were all moved on the orders of the police to Berlin. I was arrested and kept in solitary confinement in a military prison on suspicion, as I was afterwards told, of being a spy.

I slept well and had plenty of food, sent in by my stepmother. When the officer on his rounds saw me sitting on the bed eating slices of bread and butter and ham, he said, 'Just look at him sitting there and eating.' When the warder took me to empty my bucket, he said I should have stood up when the officer came in, and asked me if I hadn't been properly brought up. He told me of German victories, but I had no doubt of England's victory. He asked me what I would do if I were sent back to England, and I said that I would take a rifle and fight. He asked me if I could shoot, and I replied that I could, for I had belonged to the O.T.C. My stepmother was once permitted to visit me, and I was surprised because she seemed so small and was trembling; but I went back to my cell as if that was where I belonged. Only in the evenings, when the daylight had gone and I had sung all my German songs as I walked the four paces up and down and the one and a half paces across, did I have moments of something like fear.

After six weeks, the warder came into my cell one afternoon and said, 'You're released'. I packed my clothes and books into a soiled laundry bag, took my bowler hat, and left the prison, accompanied by a soldier. I thought he was taking me back to the pension where my stepmother and Constance were staying, but I was being transferred to the internment camp at Ruhleben.

CHAPTER III

When the soldier handed me over to the sentry at the gate, it was already dark. I was taken across to the guard-room, and by the light from tall lamp-posts I saw long low buildings with small windows and knots of ragged men standing about, whom I heard talking in a language I didn't know. They were Poles who had come to East Prussia for the harvesting; they had been arrested at the outbreak of war, and were now housed in the stables of the Ruhleben trotting race-course.

The under-officer in the guard-room rummaged in my soiled-linen bag, looked suspiciously at my Homer, tossed the bag back to me, and sent me off with a soldier to one of the low buildings. There I was handed over to another soldier, who gave me a metal bowl and spoon and an enamel mug and a horse-blanket, took me to a horse-box where three unshaven men sitting on dirty sack mattresses were playing cards, and pointed to a mattress in the corner. The three men looked up at me and said something in their unknown language. The soldier told me where to get something to eat, and I was given a piece of hard sausage. I gnawed at it as I stood beneath one of the lamp-posts.

Next morning, among the ragged prisoners standing about after an early roll-call, I saw a young man who looked like an Englishman. I caught his eye, and went up to him 'Are you English?' I asked. 'Yes,' he answered; and then said with a friendly smile, 'You look a bit lost. Come and have some breakfast.' He took me to his barrack, as the stables came to be called. Half its twenty horse-boxes were occupied by about forty Englishmen. Within a few days it was arranged with the German under-officer that I should be moved into the same barrack, and into the same horse-box as the young man, whose name was David More.

These Englishmen had already been interned several weeks. They had formed a committee to negotiate with the Germans, and had secured stools, tables and iron bunks, which were placed one above the other, in pairs, on two adjacent walls of the box, leaving a space in the middle for the table. In my box,

26

besides David More, who had come to Germany to study music, there was an engineer from Manchester, named Johnson, about twenty-six years of age, and Philips, a commercial traveller in textiles, who was a couple of years older.

In David's manner towards me there was always the friendliness of the first morning. The others treated me like a boy, and nicknamed me 'Dormouse' because, they said, I sat at the table hunched up into myself like the Dormouse in *Alice in Wonderland*. Philip asked me to give him Latin lessons, and I gladly agreed; but Johnson said that he was only studying Latin because he wanted to be a gentleman, and that I was sucking up to him. Philips asked me if I had a girl, and I thought he was impressed when I said that I had. But because they teased me, I didn't answer Lotte's letter, in which she said that though our countries were enemies, we were not; and I stopped singing my German songs.

The Germans, we said, were square-heads and Prussian bullies; defenders of 'Kultur' they called themselves – look at our pot-bellied under-officer with his shaven convict's head and the soldiers we saw at daybreak, on our way to fetch the muck they called coffee, still with the stiff gauze across their upper lip to make their moustaches turn up like the Kaiser's. They couldn't fight; the war would be over by Christmas.

Sometimes an English newspaper was smuggled in. At night, as we lay in our bunks, David More read it out in a low voice by the light of a torch hidden beneath a blanket so that the under-officer patrolling the corridor would not see the light reflected on the ceiling. Then especially, as we listened to the true news from home, hearing on the railway the rumble of trains moving German guns and troops from front to front, we felt ourselves a group of Englishmen.

Visitors were permitted, and my stepmother and Constance sat with me on the grandstand overlooking the race-course. David More was sitting with his visitor nearby; I introduced him, and he promised my stepmother that he would look after me. Next day she and Constance were to leave for Holland with the other English women and children and the men over military age, and we should be able to see the train pass as the line ran just outside the camp. At the expected time David More and I waited in the compound. The train went by with a

27

flurry of handkerchiefs, and when it had gone he laid his arm round my shoulders.

In November, some 4,000 British civilians arrived – the Polish workers had been removed some weeks previously. All the barracks were occupied, six men in each horse-box and three hundred in each hayloft. Jews were placed in a separate barrack in a remote corner of the compound.

With the increase in numbers, the Camp became a peculiar kind of society. In each barrack a captain and a vice-captain were elected, who together formed the Camp Committee under the chairmanship of the Captain of the Camp. In a short time the camp was being run by the prisoners. The German under-officers were moved out of the barracks and their rooms taken over by our captains and vice-captains; and we organized our own police force.

Though there was an intense longing for privacy – bunks were curtained off, and the secret interiors fitted with shelves for the treasures of personal life – there was the stronger compulsion of our enforced common existence. We were British prisoners of war, even though only civilians; and we must not forget it. 'Are we down-hearted?' we called out, when in the winter dawn we were lined up for the count by the German guards. 'No!' we shouted.

A poet, Dorland Smith, tall and scrawny, his Adam's apple protuberant in a skinny neck, found in our captivity religious significance. For our first Christmas he composed and had duplicated a poem, of which I remember the lines:

> Before the barred and bolted gates
> An armed and awful sentry waits;
> And all night he's waiting too
> Lest the prisoner should slip through.
> Fool! That gate is made of wood!
> Passing that would do no good.
> Follow thy soul, so pale and wan,
> Which leads thee on and ever on!

We had been vouchsafed a great experience, the poem continued: we were keeping Christmas in a stable. We had been brought back to the beginning of the Christian time. When the war was over and the gates were opened, we would go forth

28

carrying the seed that would regenerate the world. Let us humbly prepare ourselves.

A philosopher, named Dearborn, also had his circle. With three or four Oxford and Cambridge undergraduates on his either hand, he would discourse, as they walked slowly up and down beside the barbed wire fence separating the space before the grandstands from the race-track, on philosophy and life. He too believed that we were privileged: withdrawn from the impure sphere of action, we could be disinterested. Moving his hand slowly before his face, as if with the tips of his long fingers he were drawing forth the utterance from his great beaked nose, 'Life,' he intoned, 'goes on.'

When a Ruhleben Camp Magazine began to come out, as it did early in 1915, it caricatured the poet and the philosopher; and Camp gossip joked about the rivalries between the attendant 'wives'. But neither poet nor philosopher was attacked in earnest, for neither questioned that we British prisoners must say to ourselves, 'They also serve who only stand and wait'. But there were some who did not thus solace themselves. The most active was a scientist, named Thompson, employed by a firm in Berlin. He was about fifteen years older than I, though to me the difference was like that between generations. He was confident, alert, quick-moving, with capable hands, a fresh complexion and friendly green eyes, and rich, black gleaming hair, which he kept combing back with his fingers from his open and intelligent forehead.

He put up a notice on the boiler-house asking all those active in the arts and sciences and all university students, or intending students, to call at Box 10, Barrack 3.

I went to see him. I told him that I should have gone to Balliol to read classics, and he asked me where I had been to school and how I had come to be in Germany. So we got talking, and I told him about Cammin and Frau Oelgarte saying, 'Friedrich, wo ist dein Taschentuch?', at which he laughed. Then he said that besides making it possible for people like me to go on with their studies, it would be a good idea to organize concerts and plays, and he asked me if I had ever acted. I said that in the Greek play on school Speech Day, wearing my first evening dress and a false beard, I had acted Ulysses in *The Cyclops*.

29

A meeting of all those who had replied to Thompson's notice was held on the tiered benches of one of the grandstands, and the Arts and Science Union was formed, with Thompson as its chairman.

Its first success was to obtain consent from the Camp Commandant that some thirty cubby-holes beneath the grandstands, which had been used for paying out winnings on the races, should be cleared and tables and chairs put in. They were just big enough for two people to work there, and I shared Thompson's cubby-hole with him.

He read and wrote, drawing gargoyles on the margin of the page. I read the Greek and Latin texts which my stepmother had been able to send in to me, and sometimes worked at poems and humorous sketches of life in a horse-box. Often Thompson talked to me – about the difference between my childhood and his upbringing in a lower middle-class family and education at a secondary school and London University; about Shaw and Wells, Ibsen and Strindberg and Nietzsche, whose *The Birth of Tragedy* he started me reading; about the new movement in the German theatre and the future of the cinema; about his hasty marriage to a possessive wife, whom he had left for Helen.

He talked to me about the war, and told me that England was not fighting for Belgium, as I imagined. If she had thought it to her interest, she herself would have violated the neutrality of Belgium, though she would have been too clever to talk about tearing up 'a scrap of paper'. That had given Britain the pretext to display the moral indignation that Englishmen love, but Britain wasn't fighting Germany for moral reasons. She wanted to smash a business competitor. But she was making a mess of it because our generals came from public schools. They knew only what a gentleman should know, and they thought that only gentlemen should run the war. The Germans were not gentlemen, and Germany might easily win the war.

He tried to make me talk about myself; told me I was sensitive and intelligent; sent some of my poems to an American poet he knew, Sara Teasdale, who thought them promising, and encouraged me to write more. He gave me a thin green volume of poetry, *Imagistes,* and wrote my name inside; except for the red pocket-book my father had given me on the evening I had been afraid of going to hell, it was the first time I had been given a present which was not for Christmas or my birthday.

To much of what he said to me I could make little reply, except to listen. But I told him something of myself – how I had felt, when my father told us of my mother's death, that there was a little man inside me, watching to see whether I also would cry; and how I now sometimes felt that eyes were watching me, fixed on a point between my shoulder blades, so that no movement I made felt free. He said, 'Vous êtes rongé par quelque chose'.

On Thompson's initiative the Arts and Science Union in the beginning of 1915 set about producing *Androcles and the Lion*. Since Ruhleben was willy-nilly a society, he said, let us be an intelligent and active society; and for a start let us declare war on our Philistines who damned Shaw for a pro-German. I was to play Lavinia, Thompson himself the Emperor, and Dorland Smith, who had been a member of Forbes Robertson's company, played the Captain. The play was performed in what had been the refreshment room beneath one of the grandstands, the stage being built up on the long counter where the drinks had been served. Six performances, the first attended by the German Camp Commandant and his wife, were given to audiences of between three or four hundred, as mixed as the population of the Camp.

All through the day of the first performance I was in a state of trembling; but as soon as I was on the lighted stage and had spoken my first words, I was free. I stood by the footlights flirting with the 'handsome Captain', and I could see the hairs on the tip of his long thin nose. Sitting on the bare boards at the back of the stage waiting the summons to the arena and to death, I had to maintain, as I had tried to do when I received Holy Communion, an intensity of concentration in which I, as Lavinia, would live. When I spoke, imagining my heart beating beneath my breasts and my mind aware of my coming death, I had to hold the audience in the same intensity. I was being myself and not myself on the lighted stage before the dark mouth of the cavern with its dim faces. We were united, and I was safe, until the falling curtain separated us and I stood about with the other actors upon a stage emptied of its spirit.

The play was a success; and so was I, the first appearance of a woman. When we went down to the kitchens, now manned by the prisoners, the cook ladling out the soup from the great cauldron said with a grin, 'Wrap that across your chest, Lavvy. And get that Captain to marry you quick. You looked five months gone.' I didn't mind, and only feared lest they should say something which would demand of my honour that I should knock them down.

Excited by acting for the Arts and Science Union, I read Thompson's copy of Nietzsche's *The Birth of Tragedy out of the Spirit of Music*. What at school had been figures of classical mythology, Nietzsche made my own experience. In the winter mornings, when we were lined up outside the barracks for the roll-call, I liked to look at the plane trees outlined in hoar frost against the pale blue of the sky; and that was the calm pleasure of Apollonian detachment; when on windy nights I watched the constellations race through the clouds, that was Dionysian excitement. I felt that in me the Apollonian was stronger, but I wished that I was Dionysian. For the Dionysian mood, as I understood Nietzsche, was the realization of the terror of existence, and possession by that terror as by music, which I interpreted by the sensation, which occasionally recurred as I looked at a clump of trees beyond the compound, of hearing the distant pulsating throb of the deep string.

In the evenings I sometimes went to read in Thompson's box. He occupied the top bunk and had ingeniously extended it to make a kind of platform where there was just room to sit. He also took me up to another member of the committee of the Arts and Science Union, Paul Farleigh, French teacher at a school in Edinburgh, who lived in the hay-loft. Being vice-captain of the loft, he had a narrow hutch with a small window just under the roof that sloped down to within about five feet of the floor. We sat at a table by the window and talked in low voices, while at the farther end of the hutch, separated off by a horse-blanket on a string, the Scotch sailor, Bruce, who looked after Farleigh, tried to sleep. Sometimes we were joined by another member of the Arts and Science Union committee, a brilliantly versatile musician, poet and artist, with a short, pugnaciously jutting beard, named Henry Nash, who before the war had been working at an experimental theatre in Florence and knew the Italian futurists.

32

He would sit at the table and dash off savage caricatures of Dorland Smith, skinny and goose-fleshed as a plucked chicken, following his wan soul; of the Captain of the Camp as the German Emperor; and of a queue at the latrines with the caption 'They also serve who only stand and wait'.

Sometimes I did not return to my own barrack till close on midnight. Keeping an eye open for German soldiers (it was forbidden to leave barracks after 'lights out'), I crossed the deserted compound, and I was happy because this world of silent moonlight or of rain falling into a lamplit puddle and filling it with golden minnows, was my new world.

David More also went to see Thompson, and told him that he had come to Germany to study music. When the Arts and Science Union arranged for a piano to be installed in one of the rooms beneath the grandstand, he was allotted hours for practice. But he remained aloof from the other musicians in the Camp, especially those active in the Arts and Science Union, for religion meant more to him than his music.

He had the bunk above mine, and every night he crouched down on it and prayed. I admired his courage, and felt in him the power which forbade us to chaff him. In the autumn of 1914, when there had been only the few Englishmen in the Camp, he trained six or seven of us in part-singing, and on Sunday evenings he took a short service at which we sang the hymns he had harmonized and repeated the Lord's Prayer, and I felt that we belonged together. He now set himself to organize the religious life of the Camp and regularly held an evening service in a corner of one of the grandstands, to which I continued to go even after becoming friendly with Thompson and starting to read Nietzsche. An Anglican clergyman who had held a chaplaincy in Germany visited the Camp on Sundays and administered Holy Communion, and on the Saturday I used to help More to arrange the chairs in the hall beneath the grandstand, to set up altar rails, to prepare the altar itself and to decorate it with greenery. We now called each other by our Christian names.

One afternoon early in 1915, David and I were sitting alone in the box. I was reading; he was sitting at the table with a sheet of music-paper in front of him, but was writing nothing. Suddenly he got up and went out. I noticed that he was looking strange, and that it was an effort for him to push back the heavy iron door of the box. After a while I heard him returning. He stopped in the opening of the door, leaning against the wall. Then he caught hold of one of the bunks and pulled himself forward. He stood swaying, looking at me and saying nothing. 'What's the matter, David?' I asked him. He turned and lifted his arms on to his bunk and let his head fall on them. I went and stood beside him and put my arm round his shoulders. He was trembling. 'What is it, David?' I asked again. He didn't answer. I helped him to get into his bunk, and covered him with blankets, and remained standing near him. Presently Philips came in, and then Johnson. Philips fetched a medical student from a neighbouring box, who felt David's pulse and said we should let him rest. Johnson went out, saying 'I'll fetch Dearborn' – he had managed to attach himself to the string of Oxford and Cambridge undergraduates to whom Dearborn expounded the life force. He presently returned with Dearborn, who stood by David's bunk for a long moment and then sat on a stool in the corner. Huddled like a vulture, he made passes from his beaked nose. David was stirring restlessly and moaning, so I put my hand on his forehead and he grew quieter. After a short time, Dearborn left. By the time it was dark, David had fallen asleep, and we all went quietly to bed.

I had the bunk beneath David's, and presently I heard him stretch down his hand through the space between the edge of his bunk and the wall, and knew that he wanted me to take it. So I raised my arm and took it, and held it for a long time. When I felt that he was asleep, I pushed his hand up through the crack and felt it drop limply on the blanket. The next day he was better.

In the following weeks we spent much of our time together, sitting on the grandstand or on the grass beside the race-track. I read to him some of my poems. He liked them, and said with a note of sadness that it was clear what I was meant to be. I sat with him during his piano practice hours, and he explained musical form to me and showed in what different ways the same passage could be interpreted; and I was happy, and felt very near to him.

I wrote to my stepmother about him, and she wrote back

to him as well as to me, and said that we were both in her thoughts when she went to Holy Communion. David was moved and grateful. But I was conscious of deceit because I had shown myself to her as David's friend but had kept silent about Thompson.

I felt an antagonism growing between my love for David and my loyalty to the Arts and Science Union. It was now being attacked as highbrow and pro-German. After the production of *Androcles and the Lion* the Ruhleben Dramatic Society was formed. Its chairman had been assistant manager of a Berlin music-hall, and its first production was *Charley's Aunt*. But the Arts and Science Union throughout the summer of 1915 continued to produce on Monday evenings Shaw, Strindberg and Maeterlinck, in most of which productions I took part. 'Why all this highbrow stuff?' asked the Ruhleben Camp Magazine, and published caricatures of the A.S.U. 'supermen'. The attack was intensified when it was learned that Thompson was to produce Ibsen's *The Master Builder,* with George Merritt playing Solness and me as Hilda Wangel. The Arts and Science Union, it was said, were taking advantage of our being shut up behind barbed wire to shove Shaw and Ibsen down our throats. What was needed 'in a Camp like this' – a phrase which Henry Nash seized on with delight to make the theme of scurrilous cartoons – was something that everybody could enjoy, something that would take us out of ourselves. Our country was watching us (the English newspapers had stories about Ruhleben and its theatre); instead of brooding over Ibsen we must show that our spirits were high. Then with an easy mind our Government could reject Germany's proposals for an exchange of civilian prisoners, and we would be keeping the 25,000 Germans in England out of the German army and so doing our bit to win the war. But the Ibsenites didn't mind if England lost the war.

There began to be tension between David and me, for I felt that he was on the side of those whom I thought of as my enemies. I had been reading more of Nietzsche, and had now read most of Ibsen's plays. In the rehearsals for *The Master Builder* I tried to key myself up to an inner intensity as if my energy must give Solness courage to stand on the dizzy height and defy God. But when David read the play, he said

35

that it was false. The Master Builder lived on the strength which he drained from his wife; yet Ibsen made him into a tragic hero. Artists don't live on other human beings, and they don't defy God; they help us to know Him. I replied that the artist must live with the greatest possible intensity and give individual form to that experience; he was not concerned with God or religion nor with the hypocritical morality of society. I repeated what I had learned from Thompson: the talk about the war being a war for freedom and democracy and the rights of small nations was deception, in which the artist must have no part.

But when David replied that the men who were fighting believed in the ideals for which they fought, I felt what had been in my own mind as I listened to Thompson in silence: my brothers were fighting, and I wronged them by making them into the mindless instruments of politicians and financiers. And when David played to me and I looked at him, I thought that in the music and in us was a truth of which I was afraid.

We became more and more silent as we walked in the evenings beside the barbed wire fence. As we walked towards the west we could see through the meshes the setting sun, and then we turned and walked towards the darker sky.

'It's no use,' David said to me at last. 'You won't let yourself be what you are.' I remembered a phrase of Nietzsche, and replied, 'That's too easy. You have to become what you are.'

Soon afterwards David moved into another barrack, and I went no more to the religious services.

Towards the end of 1916 the Arts and Science Union published *Prisoners' Pie,* a miscellany of short stories, poems, drawings and cartoons; three of my poems were included. One of them was criticized – and I never forgot the criticism – by another contributor to the miscellany, who had done a humorous sketch of a horse-box conversation.

His name was Arch. He was the son of a printer, who was a leading Baptist in a small provincial town, and he himself had the same kind of dignity as a good craftsman. He was grave and pale, and had grown a thick dark beard, so that he looked like an Old Testament patriarch; and in his eyes

36

there was a peculiar compelling power which he was too gentle and too humorous to exercise. He told me stories of his boyhood. After leaving school at the age of eleven he had been apprenticed to a carpenter; he hated the work, and every moment that his master's eye was not on him he read poetry. One day, when he was working on a building job, he was sitting on a pile of shavings in the corner of a half-finished room, engrossed in Milton's description of Satan's flight to Earth. Suddenly he heard a loud voice and his master stood before him, huge and terrible. He was immediately sacked. Later he went to a teachers' training college and became a lay preacher, walking miles every Sunday to preach in remote villages. Then almost from one day to the next he lost his faith. He had come to Germany in reply to an advertisement for Englishmen to teach in a language school, where he was exploited by a swindling employer. He was without bitterness, but capable of intense anger against injustice to others; and he felt more than anyone I knew in the Camp the untold misery of a senseless war. Though his health was suffering, he accepted prison life with apparent equanimity and occupied much of the monotonous time reading and re-reading Dickens, chuckling to himself occasionally. There was a kindness in him which made me feel kind towards him, and we liked to be in each other's company. Though he was not much interested in Ibsen, he had been a faithful supporter of the Arts and Science Union, admired my acting, and thought I should do something notable when the war was over, though in what field he didn't know.

The poem in *Prisoners' Pie* which he criticized ran as follows:

> In splendid stream the days pass over me,
> And plunge their waters into a flaming sea:
> The spray leaps up, and breaks against the clouds.
> Madly I rush to seize it ere it falls.

Arch said to me in his quiet, grave, friendly voice: 'You never look to me to be madly rushing. In your poem you act.'

I sent *Prisoners' Pie* home, and Graeme wrote to me from the front in France, saying that he liked my poems and looked forward to meeting the poet when the war was over.

37

Not long afterwards the German authorities announced that prisoners willing to work in Germany should send in their names; if their application was accepted, they would be released. Thompson immediately volunteered. I also brought myself to the point of sending in my name. Not to do so was to take my place with the herd, standing and waiting and serving my country. I read Max Stirner's *Der Einzige und sein Eigentum*. The individual, Stirner said, is told to serve the cause of God and the State. Well, let us examine God and the State. Whose cause does God serve? His own. Whose cause does the State serve? Its own. Then let the individual follow their example and serve his own cause.

After some weeks I heard that my application to be released for work had been rejected. Thompson's was accepted, and he left the Camp early in 1917.

After he had gone, I spent more of my time with Paul Farleigh. Under his guidance I began to study French and German literature. I seldom acted any more.

For him also internment had been a time of change. His mother, to whom he was deeply attached, was a devout Catholic. She had wanted him to become a priest, and in conversation he listened to the person speaking, and his eyes behind his glasses were watchful, as if he had liked to imagine himself invested with a priest's authority and power; and his Camp nickname was 'the Jesuit'. When he talked with you, he made you feel that in this moment he wanted nothing except to know you, but that he would judge you by standards of a different order than your own. He said to me about my poems, 'They are not quite it'; and in the criticism I felt a penetration and an impersonal respect for values which Thompson's praise lacked. I felt the same qualities in his later criticism of my character: 'You are a born compromiser', and 'You are receptive to the point of weakness'.

I felt, however, that he was glad of my receptiveness. By the time I met him he was an atheist: since there was no God, the universe was without purpose; the artist must give life its meaning. In a large foolscap notebook, in which he kept a diary of his ideas, he set out what he called his 'theory of the two humanities', as distinct as if they were different species: the artists who are conscious of themselves in an otherwise

38

meaningless world, and the unconscious, contented, respectable herd. I was impressed by what I felt to be a courage that I lacked when he wrote that if anyone sneeringly said to him, 'And I suppose you think yourself one of the higher humanity', he would reply that he did. He knew that I was impressed, and I felt that he needed the assurance. Among the prisoners always going this way and that way between the barracks, we sometimes saw approaching us the black-cassocked priest with his grey beard who celebrated the Mass which Paul had in the first year or so regularly attended, and to whom he had confessed his sins; and in the tone of his 'Good morning, Father', 'Good evening, Father' I thought I heard his conscious atheism repressing fear. At night, while Bruce snored behind the blanket on the string or grumbled that we wouldn't let him sleep, Paul would talk to me about the work he was going to do; and as he leant back against the boards at the head of his bed, I thought he was like a child telling stories to his mother so that she would not go away.

In May, 1917, a letter came from my father telling me that Graeme had been killed in France. It was handed in to me while I was having tea with Paul and Henry Nash in the loft. As I raised my eyes from the letter, I saw them looking at me, and the tea-things on the table beside the low, small window looked strange and distant as if I had just recovered consciousness. I told them that my brother had been killed, and went out.

I wrote to my father, but felt that my phrases falsified my grief and the relationship between us, and my brother's death. I wrote to Cecil, who was a captain in the R.A.M.C. in Italy, and tried to tell him how much he meant to me.

During the days after the news had come, I used to go and sit on the grandstand. As the light failed, I could see in the distance beyond the race-track the blue sparks from the overhead wires of the Spandau trams; or in the daytime I could see a German plane practising loops and rolls. I waited for a stir of feeling. As I watched the prisoners criss-crossing past the wire fence, I thought that I was too small-minded to feel my brother's death.

Sometime afterwards, I was sitting in the loft of the remote barrack which had originally been set aside for the Jews and had then been cleared. From the window there was a view of a canal and waste land and factory chimneys. It was early evening, and the farther bank of the canal was reflected in the still water except where there was the dazzling of the sun. Then the sun went behind a cloud, and the reflection of a bush appeared upon the water. I thought that in this vanishing of the dazzling light and the emergence of the reflection there was an idea for a poem. Then I saw Graeme lying dead before me, as if by my thought I had caused his death.

With Thompson gone, the Arts and Science Union was moribund. I tried to emulate Paul's belief in the sole reality of the artist's vision, but I knew that it was imprisonment that gave me freedom to write poems and caused me to be housed and fed, while other prisoners, who, unlike me, got no money every month from home, brought in the coal from the railway sidings for the boiler house, and baked our pies and cakes; carted out all the refuse of the Camp, and scrubbed the bath-houses; unloaded from the trucks our parcels from England, which Bruce queued up for.

As the months went by, the spirit of the Camp became heavier. Our numbers had dwindled by the exchange of prisoners over forty-five and the release of the sick to Holland; those who remained were weary. Some had taken to handicrafts, such as carpentry, pottery and book-binding; others worked on the allotments into which we had been allowed to turn the land enclosed within the race-course. What was happening in the world outside made little impact. When the February Revolution broke out in Russia, a self-advertising journalist had given a lecture in the grandstand hall with a succession of charts on a blackboard on which had appeared in bigger and bigger letters the name of Kerensky. When the October Revolution came, I remember I said to an acquaintance, known as the 'Naturkind' because he always wore corduroy shorts and sandals and had a mane of hair and spoke German very well, 'I hope everything goes smash'; to which he replied contemptuousy, 'You talk like a flapper'.

I began to fear the ending of the war, for I would have to return to a world from which I was protected by imprisonment. I would have to face my father and tell him that I wouldn't go to Oxford, that I didn't believe in academic learning or careers, and that I was going to write. I would have to break away from home. Here in Camp I had broken with David and religion, but when I passed him on the compound and he gave me a jerky nod, I felt I had done wrong.

Reading Nietzsche, I thought I was the young lad whom Zarathustra finds wearily sitting against a tree on a hillside, and who says to Zarathustra, 'Envy of you – that has been my destruction!' In me, I thought, there is envy of Paul, who is for me Zarathustra. But stronger than uneasiness lest that envy might be my destruction, was a fear aroused by the young lad's words:

> I change myself too quickly. My today contradicts
> my yesterday. When I climb I often jump the steps,
> and that is what no step forgives me . . .

I repeated to myself, 'I have jumped a step, and that is what no step forgives me'. Then I thought, not of Paul, but of what David had said: 'You won't let yourself be what you are'.

Revolution broke out in Germany. The German officers in the Camp disappeared from their quarters, and the privates and sergeants came round the barracks saying that now we were brothers. But on the night that the Kaiser's abdication was proclaimed, a whist-drive was held in the Y.M.C.A. building put up in 1916 by the American Embassy. Since for a tin of condensed milk the sentries would open the gates and let us out, the guarding of the Camp was taken over by our own British Ruhleben police. There, I thought, you have the herd.

The evening before we were to leave for England, Thompson rang the bell at the front gate. With him was Marie, a Polish dancer whom he had married that morning. He had brought bottles of wine, and we talked and drank in Paul's cubby-hole, while those who wanted their last night's sleep shouted at us to shut up.

Next morning we were formed up and taken to the siding where the train was waiting. I found I had forgotten one of my parcels, so I ran back to fetch it. The barracks were gaunt and empty, and German soldiers were rummaging in the great heaps of litter.

41

CHAPTER IV

As the train drew in at King's Cross, in front of a pillar I saw my father. When he caught sight of me making my way towards him, he dashed forward, his arms outstretched.

He had engaged a four-wheeler from the jobbing master who had always taken us to and from the station at the beginning and end of the holidays. As we sat side by side and I smelled the familiar smell of leather and straw, I remembered how I had once watched my father's face in a small mirror let into the upholstery of the cab, not knowing that he could see mine, and suddenly the reflection had smiled at me. As the horse was plodding up the long West Hill, I said to my father, 'Let's get out and walk'. I made him stand still in a fine rain and look at the tall trees. Suddenly remembering my three imaginary children, I said to him, 'Goodnight, Grandfather'. 'Goodnight, Birt', he replied, and took my arm.

My stepmother and Constance were waiting at the lighted front door. I went towards them down the twenty yards of flagged walk from the gate on to West Hill, and wondered that they didn't come out to meet me, but supposed that it was because my stepmother would have said it was raining. Constance was grown up; and I felt that she was not happy.

The house stood unchanged. Here were the two steps down to the little recess where I hung up my coat, and to the green baize swing doors at the top of the kitchen stairs. I went down to see Fanny, who had been with us since we came to the house. We went into dinner in the long dining-room, at the end of which stood the organ my father had built.

After dinner we went into his study. My father sat with his legs stretched out towards the fender, one foot across the instep of the other, and moved the toe of the slipper in a slow circle as he looked thoughtfully into the fire; and I watched with love the familiar movement which I had forgotten.

My stepmother said, 'You'll want a complete new wardrobe for Oxford, my moley.' I thought that if I let it pass, I should be lost. So I said, 'I don't know about going to Oxford. I want to write.' There was a silence. Then my father said, 'Wait a bit, my lad. You've been out of the world for four years. Wait till Ruhleben has become a bad dream. Then you'll know what to do.' This is the beginning of the fight, I thought.

There was silence about Graeme. My stepmother held my eyes and guided them to the framed scroll hanging by the fireplace in memory of 'Capt. Arthur Graeme West', and then she looked meaningly at my father, who had not noticed.

He gripped my hand as we said goodnight. Then he unfastened his watch and chain from his waistcoat and put them in my hand. 'You are a man now, Alick,' he said, 'so you must have a gold watch and chain.'

By her manner and tone my stepmother told me that she understood me better than my father did, and that she was glad and proud that her son, as she would have had me think myself, was a poet. One morning, when she was resting in bed – for her heart was not strong – and I had gone in to talk to her, she said, as if it were our secret, 'I think you have the divine spark'. And so, as she lay back against the pillows, her grey and rather scanty hair tied back with a piece of blue tape, I walked up and down the bedroom, talking of the dawns and sunsets at Ruhleben.

I accompanied her on her morning shopping in the High Street, carrying her basket, walking on the outside next the kerb, so that she said, 'You haven't forgotten your manners'. I answered politely when we met acquaintances, and they said how terrible it must have been for me. We met a boy with whom I had been at school, now an officer with a glossy Sam Browne belt and a neat moustache, and a girl, Nancy Harvey, to whose house I had been for a dance. In the way my stepmother spoke about her after we had stood talking for some minutes, I felt her planning our engagement; and I half hoped it might happen, for I had seen in the girl's look that she liked me as I liked her. But marrying belonged to that world of the family which I had to resist.

When I was sent by my stepmother to present myself again to our neighbours, I took pleasure in saying that the Germans had treated us well, and that well-known German professors of Greek had sent me copies of their books, and that I didn't think the Kaiser should be hanged nor Germany squeezed for reparations 'until the pips squeaked'. But I knew little and

43

cared little about what was happening. I thought politicians and statesmen as unconscious as the herd they governed.

About a week after my return my father told me that he wanted to talk to me about Graeme.

From the time of joining the Army, he said, Graeme had kept a diary. Some weeks ago, shortly before the Armistice, extracts from this diary, together with some poems, had appeared as a book, under the title, *The Diary of a Dead Officer*. It had been edited by Cyril Joad, and published by the *Daily Herald* (which at that time was like a *Daily Worker*).

Joad had been my brother's close friend at Blundell's School and then at Oxford, and had frequently stayed with us during holidays and vacations. I had been fascinated by his faun-like face, his dark eyes and black hair and olive complexion, his lips like moist raspberries, and by the quick intonations of his slightly lisping voice; and I had been impressed almost to the point of awe when he said that he was an atheist. My father had not liked him. A silence had sometimes fallen on the long dinner-table when my father had contradicted him in a voice that forbade reply. My stepmother had told me to be on my guard against his 'specious cleverness'.

My stepmother had told me how deep a blow Graeme's death had been to my father. The telegram had come when my father was at work in Woolwich. When he came home, she said, one look at her face was enough. 'Graeme?' he asked; she nodded, and he had gone to his study. On its publication, Joad sent him a copy of *The Diary of a Dead Officer;* and my father read what his son had kept from him.

Untouched at first by England's declaration of war, my brother had returned to Oxford in the autumn of 1914 to do post-graduate study in English literature. This unconcerned detachment did not last, and in the Christmas vacation he applied for a commission. He was rejected on account of his eyesight; but 'more or less by ruse', as he wrote in his diary, he got himself passed by a private doctor, and in February, 1915, he enlisted as a private in the Public Schools Battalion. He crossed to France in November and was in the front line until March, 1916, when he went to a camp in Scotland to be trained as an officer.

The training was done by sergeant-majors and officers who

had never been at the front. For hours on end they marched the cadets round a field practising by numbers the correct way to salute. They told them that England was going to the dogs because discipline had got slack. The cadets must learn Prussian methods and use them on their men.

During the five months of training, my brother's outlook changed. He began to ask himself what was the purpose of the war. Then he questioned religion and patriotism.

Before returning to France as an officer, my brother had a few weeks leave, most of which he spent with Joad and his wife at Box Hill. On returning home, he was asked if he had seen his name gazetted in the papers. He wrote in his diary:

I said, 'No, I had seen no paper since I went to Dorking'. Cries of 'Graeme! Seen no paper! How can you live?'

A few days later came the summons to join his regiment. He was to report on Monday, August 21. On the previous Saturday he went down to see Joad for the last time, returning home in the evening.

Never was the desire to desert and commit suicide so overwhelming, and had it not been that I knew I would pain many people, I would certainly have killed myself that night . . .

. . . I stayed up late and read B. Russell's *Justice in War Time* and went to bed so impressed with its force that I determined to stand out openly against re-entering the Army.

Next day he wrote to the Adjutant of the Battalion

telling him that I would not rejoin the army nor accept any form of alternative service, that I would rather be shot than do so, and that I left my name and address with him to act as he pleased.

Shortly after midnight I went down to the post with this letter and two more, one to J . . . , one to E . . . , telling them what I had done. I stood opposite the pillar-box for some minutes wondering whether I would post them – then put them in my pocket and returned home to bed.

On the following day he rejoined his regiment.

My father persuaded himself that this was not the real voice of his son. He felt certain, he said to me, that Joad had acted against Graeme's wishes in publishing these personal papers. When Graeme had written what he had written, he had not been himself. If he were alive today, he would repudiate the book.

He made it clear that he did not wish me to read the book nor to have anything to do with Joad. But I went to see him, and he gave me a copy, which Constance then also read; and she and I came nearer to each other.

When Constance and I were left alone after Graeme and Cecil had gone away to boarding school, we used to play together in the garden of the house in Holly Terrace. There was a large walnut tree which we used to climb, and on the rough grass we tried to waltz on stilts. In one rather dark corner, beside some dank laurel bushes, the earth sloped up into a mound against the dividing wall, and down this slope we used to career in Constance's old doll's perambulator, seeing who could recite most of a certain passage from a book called *Katawampus* before the perambulator came to a stop. Later we used to go out and play cricket on Parliament Hill Fields when we had got back from afternoon school. At Christmas time, when Constance went to parties, I used to call for her and bring her home, carrying by the string the holland bag with her best slippers. Sometimes I helped her with her homework. One evening when I was doing my own 'prep' in the playroom after dinner, Constance came quietly in her nightgown and asked me to take round to her school before I went to bed some homework of hers; and when I said I would, she smiled happily and danced out of the room. At mealtimes we teased each other under our stepmother's permissive eye. We were often sent out by her between lunch and afternoon school to leave 'little notes' at the houses of acquaintances or to hand in parcels of old clothes to the poor families in Southwood Lane, where my stepmother regularly called as District Visitor from St. Michael's Church; and we grumbled to each other about our stepmother's mania for organising. Constance later told me that she resented having me held up to her as a model because I was 'good'; and I resented being told that a boy should be the chivalrous protector of his younger sister. When we were

46

out together and met boys from my school, I wished Constance were not there; for under the boys' eyes I blushed. Yet we were glad to be brother and sister, and in each other's company we were free from family repression – and Constance, being so much younger and a girl, had had to submit to rule and management by our stepmother far more than we boys.

After reading Graeme's book, I understood more what she had suffered by his death.

I think that Graeme must have had an unusual sense of responsibility towards Cecil and me and towards Constance. When Constance was shut up in her room in the night-nursery with measles or chicken-pox and we could not see her, Graeme used to write her nonsense letter and stories and send them in to her with our nurse, Miswuz. I have related how he said to me that he would speak to Father if I didn't stop my self-induced crying. It was he who first told Cecil that he should become a doctor, and that he would do well in life – in which he was quite right, for Cecil became a Professor of Anatomy, respected and loved by generations of his students.

I think Graeme did what he could to stand between us and our father. I remember him saying to me that when my father was whipping Cecil or me in the study at Talbot Road where in fearful silence we had all been doing our homework, he wanted to throw himself on our father and tear the strap away from him, which made me aware that I felt no such anger, but rather watched with pleasure and went over to my father's side.

When he had gone to Oxford, he did not separate himself from us, but wanted us to share his new life. To break through the family silence in which the evenings ticked away, he started us reading Shakespeare's plays – my stepmother, for reasons incomprehensible to me, suddenly coughing and jumping a line. Despite her protests at its unsuitability, he took me to see *Fanny's First Play*, and he talked to me about literature and philosophy as if we were equals.

So, I imagine, during the first years of the war, he wanted to give Constance, then in her mid-teens, something of the happiness she had a right to. She had been sent by our step-mother to Cheltenham College, where the girls had to knit balaclava helmets while *The Times* was read aloud. In his

47

letters to her and in their few meetings Graeme lightened for her the oppression of this regimented world. Among the poems printed in *The Diary of a Dead Officer* was one which my brother had written after he and Constance had spent a long summer's day together in the country during one of his periods of leave. They had missed their train back to London, and until the next one came they had lain down in a hayfield and read ballads to each other.

> The year was at the summer's spring
> When grass is fresh and long,
> And flowers are more in bud than bloom,
> And cuckoos slacken song . . .
>
> The hawkweed on our ballad book
> Sprinkled its pollen fine,
> And now and then a beetle dropped
> And wandered through a line . . .

On the day that Graeme returned to France for the last time, he and Constance were for some hours alone in the house. He talked to her and, as he wrote in his diary, 'let her see something of what was in my mind'.

When the news came of his death, she had to bear alone her loss and the half-knowledge that he had been killed in a war which he thought wrong.

She and I came closer to one another in talking about him. I also showed her my poems, which she liked, and talked to her about wanting to write – she herself was soon going to Cambridge to study French and Italian.

But I could not give to her what Graeme had given. He had wanted to help her to live freely what was in her and to be part of the life which war could not kill. Though I had been moved on the first evening when I saw that she was unhappy, I didn't want thus to help her. I repeated to myself a line from Hofmannsthal *The Fool and Death* which I had read in Ruhleben: Das Trösten hab'ich nie gelernt – I have never learned to comfort; for the lack of this power was proof that I shared the Fool's and the artist's isolation. Similarly in reading Graeme's book I fastened particularly on passages expressing the kind of mood which, when I experienced it, made me think well of myself. I often repeated to myself a sentence he wrote when he returned home after staying on his last leave with Joad and his wife: 'Strong upon me to-night, with M . . . 's laugh and J . . . 's voice far away, is the now familiar feeling of unreality'.

I criticized him, however, in my mind because he did not hold to this sense of unreality. There appeared a review of the book in *The Times Literary Supplement*, under the heading 'A Hamlet of the War', which said that Graeme 'lacked entirely the herd-instinct'. After his return for the last time to France he had written in his diary:

Had I stood apart I should have stood on firm logical ground; where I was truth would have been, as it is among my friends now.

To defy the whole system, to refuse to be an instrument of it – this *I* should have done.

That, I though, was herd-instinct disguised; it was not for the artist either to serve or defy a system to which only the herd accorded reality.

But one evening when Constance and I were sitting in the playroom and I was reading Graeme's book, I was suddenly smitten with the knowledge that he was dead. I felt a nervous constriction in my breast, and crying out, 'I can't stand it', I threw myself down beside Constance's chair. During the seconds that I remained crouching there, I knew that though the constriction of grief had been real, I had had the choice between crying out and not crying out, and that I had let myself cry out because, as Arch said, I was acting. I did not want to help Constance as Graeme had done; I wanted her to pity and comfort and admire me.

When after this partly artificial spasm of sorrow I imagined Graeme standing with the letters in his hand before the pillar-box, unaware that the silence of midnight around him made all action meaningless, I felt, though I could not have said why, as if I was betraying him.

My father and I did not speak any more of Graeme nor of his book, but I felt that for my brother's sake I must not weaken towards my father.

D   49

At first there were moments of nearness between us. On the evening of the first day after my return, he said when he got home from his work at Woolwich Arsenal, 'All day I've been walking on air!' He got time off, and took me to his tailor in the City, and fitted me out with two suits and evening dress. He took me down to his bank in the Archway Road, introduced me to the manager and told him I wanted to open an account, to which he transferred the income of the shares left me by my mother – amounting to about £90 a year – since I had come of age. On fine Saturdays and Sundays in the next two or three weeks we went for walks in the country, which still began just beyond East Finchley, though we noted how London had spread since the days before the war, when from Church End out beyond Barnet and westwards to Rickmansworth we had got to know the country so well, giving our own names to footpaths and streams and farms, that we felt as if we had a kind of proprietary right in it. My father now recalled these walks, and I responded, for I had enjoyed them. He talked also about his war work. On the back of an envelope, as we sat in a country pub having our cheese and beer, he drew a sketch of the mechanism of a shell, with sure strokes of his beautifully sharpened pencil, and I watched with something of the same pleasure as when I had stood beside him at his bench in his workshop when he was mending or making something for the house, and I handed him screws or nails, and he had whistled softly and tunefully. Once he asked me if I remembered my mother, and I told him my few memories, and he said that he was glad that I had them. Though we had not yet talked any more about what I was going to do, he showed that it was in his love for me that he wanted to hear and listen and advise me. One rather grey Sunday afternoon we were walking by the grass verge of a road near Edgware. A little way off to the left was a copse of silver birches; and as we moved, so did the trees. As in a dance, they slowly circled, passing behind and in front of each other, shining forms in the dark wood. 'Look,' I said to my father, and pointed to the copse. He saw what I meant, and stopped, and I with him; and all was still. Then, holding my arm, he walked me on; and the movement began again. When it was left behind, my father said, 'It's a beautiful world'; and I knew he was thinking of

50

God. Presently he asked, in friendly, interested enquiry, 'Could you write a poem about that?' 'I could try,' I said.

He said to me one day – I was sitting on the floor beside him in his study – 'I feel I've made a sad mess of my life'. I put my hand on his knee, and said, 'I know what you mean, Father; and I'm very sorry for you'. When he was young, I thought, he must have wanted, like me, to be himself, and he had been defeated. What he had achieved – the years with my mother, bringing up with her in the fear and love of God the children she had borne him, slowly playing religious music on the organ he had built with his own hands – was almost gone. The family I had first known was still being destroyed by death, war and change, and now by me, who would not recognize our relationship of father and son but was proud of the emotion with which I laid my hand on his knee.

At last, one evening early in January, 1919, when I had been home rather more than a month, my father said to me, 'Well, my dear lad, what are you going to make of your life?' I said again that I wanted to write. 'What will you live on?' he asked me. I said that I could manage on the money my mother had left me, and that I ought to be able to make a little more by writing. There was no reason, my father said, why I shouldn't write; but wouldn't it be wise to have a second string to my bow? For I should find it very hard to manage on the money left me by my mother, and one day I might want to marry. There was nothing like having a good university degree behind one, so why not go to Oxford? Then if I found I couldn't live by my writing, or if I found I had made a mistake, I could still make a useful and honourable career for myself. I said that I thought you had to choose; if you tried to make a career, you were recognizing a set of social values which had nothing to do with poetry. Poetry meant being aware of living, not of careers. And I thought Oxford would be bad for me; it was an institution for turning out English gentlemen. The Oxford professors knew nothing about literature because they never tried to live what they read. Even if I was right, my father said, why should I be afraid of Oxford? Why couldn't I go there and get the degree I needed, and stick to my guns? 'A man ought to be captain of his soul,' he said. If I didn't go, I should be cutting myself off from life. 'A man must make others listen,' he said.

51

'He must speak out the truth that is in him.' Those words stuck.

My father tried to find somebody else whom I might listen to. A distant cousin was lecturer in English at Cambridge, so my father asked me to send him some of my poems. I did so, and we then went to see him. He though my work showed promise; but 'a self-conscious poet,' he said, 'is a lost soul. Of that I am convinced.' On the way home my father asked me if I didn't agree with him. I replied that a poet must be above everything else self-conscious. Then my father took me to a nerve specialist, who said I needed a long rest; so my father asked me if I would go to another cousin of ours who was farming in Canada. I said I wouldn't.

My stepmother might be happy that she could see in me 'the divine spark', but her loyalty was to my father and to the family. Though her different tradition made her a stranger among us, she had devoted herself, since she married my father, to making a house into a home and a widower and his four children into a family around herself. Now the home she had made was filled with enmity between a father and a son to whom she mattered little. She appealed to me not to go against what my father wished, and wished only for my own good. She would not speak of herself, she said; it was far worse to see how the one you loved was suffering night and day. Why would I not go to Oxford? Had not Graeme been to Oxford? And when I met the girl I wanted to marry, how should I feel when I had to remain silent because I couldn't offer her a home? When she found me unmoved, she said, 'You are wrapped in a cocoon of self-conceit, which I mean to rend in order that you may see the light'.

Thompson had a job in London, and he and Marie had come to supper one evening. Marie had charmed my stepmother with a story of her romantic life, related in broken English, though between Thompson and my father there had been argument about Germany. I now went to see them frequently in the evenings, and Thompson encouraged me not to give way. 'Your father,' he said, 'has all the possessive instincts of the middle class; he thinks of a son as a piece of property.' At breakfast, my stepmother would formally ask if I proposed to be in for dinner. When I was there, my father and my stepmother conversed resolutely as if I were not present, and Constance was silent. Once my father happened to say that the Germans should never be forgiven for their atrocities; and I banged the table, and in a voice I had never heard myself use said that the German atrocities were nothing to those of the British when in the Mutiny we had tied Indians to the muzzles of our guns and blown them to pieces.

As I now often came home after my father and my stepmother had gone to bed, and didn't come down to breakfast before he left for Woolwich, I would sometimes find beside my plate with its pattern of pink rose-buds a note from him. One morning he had written that he suspected from something I had let drop that I might be thinking of selling out my capital; and he thought it only right to warn me that if I did so he would cut me out of his will, for I should have shown myself unfit to be trusted with the control of money. Theobald Pontifex, I thought, in *The Way of All Flesh,* shaking his will at Ernest.

I told Thompson of the threat, and he then asked me what my father was going to do with Graeme's share of the money left us by our mother; legally, he said, it should be divided between Cecil, Constance and me, so I should ask my father for my share.

I nerved myself to speak one evening as my father was going upstairs to bed and I was in the hall. My father turned round on the stairs, 'Graeme died intestate and left his money to me'. And he started upstairs again. I said, and my father stopped, his knee bent, 'I thought that the meaning of intestacy was that the property was not left to anyone'; and I heard in my voice a bored superiority. My father rushed down a few steps, and said, 'His property comes to me as next-of-kin', then turned and went on up to the bedroom.

Next morning there was a note from him beside my plate, saying that I must either obey him or leave the house by the end of the week. After dinner on the Friday evening – for though I was decided, I waited – we all went into the drawing-room, and Fanny brought in the coffee on a silver tray. As she went out again, she exchanged a look with me from the door; for we were fond of each other, and she guessed something of what was happening.

My father finished his coffee. After he had put down the cup,

53

he extended his right arm in front of him, slanting it downwards. Since I was a child, I loved his hand – warmly freckled, strong and friendly, with the intelligent fingers of a craftsman. He moved it a little, curving and straightening the fingers. 'What a strange thing a hand is!' he said. I knew well that he had moments of fascinated interest in the wonder of living things; but knowing what I was presently going to say to him and believing that he knew also, I said to myself, 'You have no right to do that now'.

At the usual time, about ten o'clock, my stepmother and Constance went up to bed. My father waited till they had been gone a few minutes, then closed his book and knocked out his pipe on the grate. 'Well,' he said, 'which is it to be?' 'I'm not going to Oxford,' I said. 'So be it,' he replied. 'You will leave the house on Monday.'

Next day my father said that my stepmother had suggested I might be ready to go to Trinity College, Dublin. Taken aback I asked for time. 'No,' said my father. 'You must give me your answer tomorrow.'

I said that I would go – perhaps because I hadn't the energy to start the fight again when the climax had come and gone, or because I could say to myself that Ireland was not Oxford.

CHAPTER V

Coelum non animum mutant qui trans mare currunt: that was
one of my few Latin tags. I had run across the sea and was
under the gentler Irish sky, but that was the only change.

Not even outwardly had I broken with the family. Outside
Dublin, in Kingstown, as Dun Laoghaire was then named, lived
my stepmother's sister, whom we had been told to call 'Auntie
May'. She lived in a large, grey, square, stone house named
Ellerslie, which came to have in my eyes the same appearance
of established permanence as Trinity College. The University
stood at the junction of the busiest streets of Dublin, separated
from the traffic and the clanging trams of the alien city by high
railings and a narrow strip of grass; from the jostle of the pavement you turned off into the front entrance with its uniformed
and watchful porter and then through an archway like a short
tunnel into a large square of dignity and quiet. Here there was
loyalty to England, as there was at Ellerslie, where I was expected to spend Sundays.

I went every three or four weeks. Auntie May treated me
kindly but firmly, as if I were not quite well or not quite sane;
and as she sat erect in her bombazine dress, darning my socks,
she told me to join the T.C.D. tennis club and take part in the
life of the college, instead of moping in my room and ruining
my health.

I was taking classics, with six or seven other men and two
girls, to whom none of us men ever spoke as we stood at the
top of the stone staircase, waiting for the professor to open his
door. The lectures were dully academic, but I did the necessary work. I became friendly with a farmer's son from the west
of Ireland, who frankly said that he was studying only in order
to get a post in the Civil Service so that he would be able to
keep his parents when they were old.

I went for long walks in the Wicklow mountains, and sometimes sang my old German songs. As I sat on a hummock in
the gorse and bracken, I looked back over the land to Dublin
and out across the Irish Sea, and tried to feel in myself the
space and the silence. Then the mood ebbed, and I became

55

conscious of the ground I was sitting on and of my body. As I dug at the peaty soil with the heels of my shoes, of which Auntie May said I didn't take proper care, I felt the mass of the earth and remembered one of Nietzsche's recurring phrases, 'the spirit of heaviness'.

One Sunday morning when I was staying at Ellerslie for the week-end, I went early before breakfast to Killiney Bay. It was a fresh, bright morning after a night of storm, the long waves rolling in; and the Wicklow mountains were clear in the distance. The beach was deserted, so I bathed naked and then ran up and down the sand. Later in the day I wrote a poem, of which I liked to repeat to myself the first verse:

> The waves run high.
> Breaking, they hurl their spray,
> Pure, glistening white,
> Into the morning.
> Happy, happy am I
> Before the face of the day.

I had great pleasure also when Auntie May's married daughter came to stay at Ellerslie with her two children, a girl and a boy, Honor and Michael, aged seven and five. I rigged up a platform in a tree in the garden, and we used to climb up and have picnics. One day when I was cleaning their mother's bicycle and I got irritated with Honor because she wouldn't stop twiddling the back wheel, she said with friendly scorn, 'Cross idiot', which I thought was very like me. When they were in bed, I used to tell them fairy stories; one evening when Michael had, as usual, asked to see my father's gold watch and I had pressed the spring, making the cover fly open, he gazed at the face and then said to me gravely, as if he were telling me something I didn't know but ought to, 'It's God that makes the long time, and only the angels in Heaven know how wonderful He is.'

Late that same evening I was riding back to Dublin on the top of the tram. From the seat behind me I heard a man's voice saying defiantly 'Let them march their armies up the country and down the country . . . ' and the rest was lost in the rattling and creaking of the tram. Turning to the window, I could see the reflection of his face in the darkness outside, like an accompanying spectre.

In the summer vacation I went home. My father said no word about the past; and we tried unsuccessfully to tune the organ he had built.

In the autumn of that year, 1919, Paul came to Dublin. His brother, a couple of years younger than he, was carrying on some kind of export and import business with Germany, and he wanted Paul's help with the language. It wasn't much of a job, but Paul didn't want to go back to teaching, and he thought that Dublin would be more lively than Edinburgh and living alone on his parents.

He now began writing prose poems on 'the immensities and the eternities' and a long essay on the nihilistic pessimism of Synge's plays. But though he was still treating the same kind of theme as in Ruhleben, in manner and mood he was far more lively. He was immensely stimulated by women, who found him fascinating. In all social behaviour he was far more enterprising than I. Within a short time of his arriving in Dublin, he had gone round to the Abbey Theatre, talked to Lennox Robinson about the Arts and Science Union's 'experimental theatre' in Ruhleben, and got to know Lord Dunsany, A.E. and other writers; and he made me come with him to their evenings.

In order not to leave me in the background, he spoke about my poems and acting; and so I was asked to play at the Abbey Theatre, and for the first time I acted men's parts. I played the elderly clerk in Shaw's *Augustus Does His Bit*, a part in one of Dunsany's plays, and Chechov's *A Tragedian in spite of Himself* – one long monologue of a harassed husband loaded by his wife with commissions, who unburdens himself to a friend, and the friend only gives him another commission to take down into the country a sewing-machine and a canary in a cage. I repeated in a dead mumbling voice 'A sew-ing Ma-chine? A ca-Nary in a Cage?' Then I had to go wild; shouting 'I want blood! I want blood!', I chased my tormentor off the stage.

I greatly enjoyed it, and I sent home the notices about me in the *Irish Times*, and my father warned me not to burn the candle at both ends. Yet I didn't mind if I never acted again.

And though A.E. was kind and said some pleasant words about my poems, yet since I didn't think much of his own poetry I wasn't stirred. Despite Paul's efforts to bring me in, I rarely became part of the evening. I was too ignorant to follow the political discussions about the liberation of Ireland from British rule, and too shy and self-centred to ask questions. I was most at ease when I went to the house of a lady to whom Oscar Wilde, by means of the ouija-board, was dictating a comedy – 'We are on the second act,' she told me – and I was pleased when she said that I was a good medium and that her control liked me.

I continued to read Nietzsche and made notes on such sayings as

Memory says, 'I did that'; pride says, 'I can't have done it'. Memory at last gives in.

I had thought that despite Freud – whose *Interpretation of Dreams* and *Psychopathology of Everyday Life* I had read in Ruhleben – I didn't suppress unpleasant memories. But this aphorism made me suspect that, just as there are murders done and never known, so beneath my quiet manner there was a power for evil of which I was unaware. 'Try free association,' I thought, and into my mind came this memory: I was about ten, and it was morning break at the prep school; a boy, named Kiddy, was standing with his back to me at the top of a bank that sloped steeply from the playground to a field; I pushed him, and he rolled down, and I walked away; when we had returned to our classroom, the master asked who was the boy who had pushed Kiddy down the bank; I stood up; 'You might have broken his back,' said the master; I sat down. There is somebody in literature, I thought, whom I am very like, and remembered Blifil in *Tom Jones*.

I also described in my notes how one evening when I was at supper in Hall among the chattering, knife-clattering, bread-throwing, loyal, healthy herd, I thought, 'At any moment I want, I can slew myself round, cock my leg over the bench, walk down between the long tables, and out at the great door'. Then suddenly I realized that I couldn't. Being what I was, I would sit there. It had no sense to say with Zarathustra, 'Become what you are', for I was already myself, bound by cause and effect.

Early in 1920 I began to work for a classical scholarship. One evening I was working late in my rooms in College. On the table was a reading lamp which had belonged to Graeme. The lamp itself could be moved up and down on a vertical rod and adjusted to the right height, and the oil flowing down to it through a tube from a cylindrical container, gurgled at regular intervals. Suddenly, from not very far away, came the sound of shots. I counted, and made a note on my paper: *1.10 a.m. five shots,* as if my evidence might be required at a trial. In my mind's eye I saw the body of a policeman, one of the Royal Irish Constabulary, famous, as Auntie May used to say, for their height, lying on the pavement in the light of a nearby street-lamp, his helmet in the gutter. Since the shots there had not been a sound, except the gurgling of the lamp.

I used this to end a sketch, published in the *Manchester Guardian,* of which the opening was the voice I had heard on the tram coming back from Ellerslie. As I wrote it and tried to deepen the silence after the shots, I thought of my brother standing at midnight before the pillar-box with the unposted letter and felt that I was misusing the memory.

I got my scholarship, as did two of the other men in the class and both the girls. We didn't congratulate the girls; but one of the men who had failed to win a scholarship, son of a leading Dublin estate agent, boasted to us that he had written an anonymous letter to one of the girls accusing her of cheating at the examination. I was very angry; and next morning, as we waited in our separate groups at the professor's door, I went up to her and said that we wished to congratulate her on her scholarship and that we would see that the man who had insulted her wrote a letter of apology – which he did. After that, I used to walk beside her across the quadrangle after lectures; and I was ready to fall in love. But the term came to an end and nothing had happened.

Not long afterwards, as I lay in bed one morning, I coughed and felt something in my mouth, and there on my handkerchief was a clot of blood. I was frightened and excited. I went home, anticipating blame from my father and stepmother, as if getting ill were the foreseeable result of my behaviour. But they were anxious and had me thoroughly examined. There was no cause for alarm, but I should not spend the winter in England. I was glad, and said to Constance, 'I shall have six months freedom'.

My stepmother's brother was a professor of medicine at Cairo University and acquainted with Flinders Petrie; so it was arranged that I should join an archaeological expedition that was being sent out from London University and winter in the desert. I went every day to the Egyptology Department to get a smattering of hieroglyphs and pot-dating; and in October, in thick fog, the steamer moved slowly down the Thames.

After twelve days we reached Alexandria. Arab porters in long robes and sandals swarmed on to the deck, shouting and gesticulating. Like snakes, hands with purple palms darted and seized my bags, and I followed down the ladder and was rowed across the smooth green water.

From the balcony of my uncle's flat I looked across Cairo to the surrounding desert. Everywhere on the flat roofs you could see people and strings of washing; kites were continually circling in the unfamiliar high blue sky; and there was an indefinable smell, as of dry refuse and hot stone. The glaring streets were noisy with trams and the shouts of the drivers of the open horse-drawn carriages, and crowded with Greeks, and Italians, and Egyptians in red hats, and Arabs and Nubians in turbans, and veiled, black-skirted women, walking with the unhurrying gait of cows. I turned off into side-streets, teeming with human beings, and turning another corner I was in a narrow alley, where in doorways and windows and low balconies, sitting, sprawling, silent and screaming, everywhere were women. For the first time I saw naked breasts. A man and a woman grabbed me each by an arm. I shook them off.

The archaeological expedition was in charge of Leslie Hynes, a man about ten years older than I, who, when I first met him, was still in the uniform of a British captain. The site was about two hundred miles up the Nile. On the edge of the desert was a ruined pyramid of the 12th dynasty; its chambers had already been opened the previous year, but beneath a smaller unfinished pyramid there might be a queen's burial chamber, and the expedition was to search for it. Shafts were to be sunk at two opposite corners and tunnels driven from them to meet underneath the pyramid. About twenty men were

60

engaged from neighbouring villages. Hynes and his wife slept in what he thought to be the entrance to an unfinished tomb cut out of the rock in the precincts of the pyramid, and I in another. The men made an encampment, with three or four donkeys, about a hundred yards off.

We got up at sunrise, and the morning light was clear and pure over the desert. The pyramid, built around a core of limestone with bricks made from the mud of the Nile, now worn away into a shapeless black mound, stood on a slight rise a few hundred yards away from the edge of the cultivated land. Over the Nile valley, across which one could see to the hills of the eastern desert, lay a morning mist, out of which rose grey shadowy palm trees around invisible villages. Moment by moment the mist dispersed and the colours of the vegetation became as clear as the light on the desert, where rivulets of lemon sand ran between shoals of purple flints, and the blue sky soared, and I was happy.

After breakfast, the work was set going on the sinking of the shafts – the rock was soft and chipped easily. Then Hynes and I, with black and white measuring rods, compass and camera, went out with a party of men and boys into the desert.

When the shafts had been sunk sufficiently deep and the tunnels were being driven, I climbed down each evening to measure how much the men had cut and with compass, string and candle to check the orientation so that the tunnels would meet. Then we had supper beside the unfinished pyramid, played bridge and broke up early.

By the light of a hurricane lamp I read and made notes for a couple of hours and wrote long letters to Paul. Sometimes I thought of the spot on my lung below my right collar-bone but neither feared nor hoped to be ill. Before going to bed, I went out into the desert beyond the pyramid precincts. Against the night sky the pyramid looked like the skull of an ape, and there was the faint sound of the wind around it. Sometimes I climbed up the track worn over the years by the women from the villages, who, it was said, believed that if they lay down on the summit of the pyramid they would conceive. Once, all the circle of the desert was bright in the moonlight. As a cloud covered the moon, all became dark. Then the moon came out, and the desert flowered again, and I remembered how my father had said that the world was beautiful. On our free days I used to walk to a great core of limestone that cropped out from the desert, climb the slope of fine sand piled up around it from its weathering, break off a piece of rock, throw it down the slope and listen to the thin hiss of sand that trickled after it till all movement ceased.

Inertia reigned, and the continual sun. Beneath the expanse of desert towards the Nile were the graves which the unknowing successors of the dead would clear of the sand and silt of centuries. Then Hynes' electric torch, searching the darkness of a burial chamber at the bottom of a deep shaft, shone upon wrapped bodies lying all over the floor beneath the low ceiling, and picked out among them a wooden coffin lid, with a white face painted on it, on which a slab of rock had fallen just below the neck, its weight forcing the lid upwards, so that it looked as if a sick woman were painfully raising her head. We searched for rings and beads among the dust of the bodies, and then the skulls and bones were passed up in baskets and emptied around the mouth of the shaft by the boys. When there was nothing more to be examined and a plan of the grave had been made with its orientation, the bones were thrown down the shaft again, and as they clattered against the rock and the dust still clinging to them rose in brown clouds, the small boys shouted and danced.

I liked to watch, but I wasn't interested in the work of the expedition, though I made a show of interest to Hynes. For behind him was the British army, whose uniform he had worn. Every day *The Times* arrived, and when there was news of the killing of British officers in Ireland, Hynes and his wife used the same language as my stepmother's sister. Again I said nothing; and I thought that although I had spoken to Constance of a time of freedom, I was no more free than at home.

The men hewing the tunnels sometimes injured themselves, and I used to dress their cuts; and I had picked up enough Arabic to talk to them a little. Their manner with me was more familiar than with Hynes; and one day, as they were excavating a shallow grave, one of them who had been taking a short rest as he leaned back against the side of the grave and chatted to me, unwrapped a loaf of bread from his discarded outer garment on the sand beside him and gave it to me. Then he saw

Hynes approaching and made gestures to me to hide the loaf. 'I can't have a secret with an Arab,' I thought; so when Hynes came up, I said, 'Ali gave me this loaf'. I was conscious that I had acted as an Englishman; and I was conscious of the separation between us and the Arabs when I looked at the boys waiting beside the men for the baskets to be filled, their eyes ringed with crawling flies; and travelling in a first-class carriage to the nearest town to buy some camping equipment, I saw held up outside the window, as the train halted at a station, the stump of a small brown arm, the hacked bone protruding, and a child's voice whined for money.

When the tunnels beneath the pyramid had met and hope of finding a burial chamber had been abandoned, Hynes and his wife joined the main expedition under Flinders Petrie, and I decided to go up the Nile to Luxor and Assuan.

I saw avenues of sphinxes leading to temples, and colossal statues of seated gods, their hands and forearms flat on their thighs, solitary in the cultivated land, while the peasants went on hoeing the earth as if the statues were erratic blocks of stone in the middle of their fields. Often I rode out on a donkey to the hills and the Tombs of the Kings, an Arab running at my side, cheapening the price of a fake antique. I liked most the temple of Queen Hatshepshut with its colonnades of white pillars at the foot of the cliffs of red rock. But when I emerged into the sunlight from the darkness of the tombs, my mind was exhausted by the riot of their incomprehensible gods and goddesses, alligators, jackals, dogs and cows and cats which had been flicked into being in the light of a bare electric bulb.

I returned to my uncle's flat in Cairo. Himself unmarried, he shared it with a Dr Francis and his wife, who did the housekeeping and ordered the most excellent meals. It was my uncle, however, who ruled the household; and he imposed upon the white-robed red-sashed servants such respect for his authority that they seemed to read and instantly obey his thoughts.

As a boy, I had thought him a most wonderful man. He had given me an unbelievable day at the Anglo-French Exhibition at the White City, taken me on the Flip-Flap and the Great Wheel, filled me with strawberries and cream and ices, and brought me home in a taxi. With mounting awe I watched the rising sum in the taxi-meter, while my uncle would suddenly burst into the popular song 'Oh, I'm glad I am back in Paree, No more of the Flip-Flap for me!' – for he could suddenly become very gay and as suddenly turn unaccountably serious. Now, seeing him ten years later, I thought that there must have been some crisis in his life and suspected that, even if, as my stepmother was fond of saying, he had the hands of a surgeon, he had never wanted to be a doctor; and I felt it particularly when I came in and heard him improvising, with a beautifully round and warm touch, on his grand piano. He always stopped when he heard me, and we never had any but the most superficial conversation. I wished I could have talked to him. I gave him some music; but his manner of accepting it seemed to tell me that he would never play from it. I felt that, though he had thought me a nice boy, he now did not like me. Having disciplined himself to renounce completely whatever he had wanted to do as a young man – on the fly-leaf of one of his books, without any relation to the contents, I found written in the beautiful script he had fashioned for himself, Goethe's phrase about the necessity of renunciation, *Entbehren sollst Du, sollst entbehren* – he thought me lacking in discipline, conceited and bad-mannered. He had rigorously excluded from his mind any questioning of his family's code of the English garrison in Ireland, and now, with a consciousness much stronger than my stepmother's had ever been, he was part of the British garrison in Egypt.

So between us was all that my stepmother would have told him about me, and his own percipience of our antagonism. Being his sister's stepson and in his flat, I was in his charge; but I was neither kinsman nor guest. My father had told me that he had arranged with my uncle for him to defray my expenses; and when I asked for money, my uncle gave it to me without question. But in order that I should not have to ask him so often and that my father should not know how much I was spending, I wrote to the bank in Highgate to send me £25 post restante. And if, when I wrote, I did not know why I wanted it, I soon found out.

For a couple of hours after breakfast I wrote descriptions of the desert, the pyramid and the excavating, the temples at Luxor and the tombs in the Valley of the Kings. I spent a long time in the museums of Egyptian art and visited the old mosques, where in the loose canvas slippers I was made to tie over my shoes I shuffled round uneasily beneath the looks of those for whom the place was holy.

At night I approached deviously the street of the brothels, but always turned back. One night, however, in one of the main streets, an open horse-drawn carriage was coming towards me and leaning back in the corner was a young Egyptian woman. I heard her call to the driver, and when I looked back the carriage had stopped. I turned and walked to it and got in, persuading myself that she was not a prostitute. After many turnings through obscure alleys, the carriage stopped outside a low house. We went into a room and she put her arms round me. I heard a slight noise, and opening my eyes, over her shoulder I saw the door open a few inches and an old skinny hand glide in like a snake's head and place two neatly folded little towels on the curved edge of the wooden washstand, and withdraw itself and close the door. So now I knew, and gave her £2. Then I kissed her and embraced her brown body with delight.

As we dressed again, she called out something, and the old woman brought two glasses of spirit, and we drank each other's health. The carriage was still there; so she must have known, I thought, that we wouldn't be long. We drove back into the centre of Cairo, and she was friendly and gay, and told me that the Arabic for sweetheart was *habibi,* and asked me, laughing, when I would come again to do *zig-a-zig;* and while I was with her, I also felt careless.

But when she had dropped me and I was walking back to the flat, I began to be afraid of infection; and finding a chemist's shop open, I bought permanganate of potash (in my uncle's files of the *British Medical Journal* I had read a long correspondence on preventive disinfection). To my relief the flat was empty, and I washed myself all over in my uncle's bath.

As I lay in bed under the mosquito net, I said to myself 'Thou shalt love thy neighbour as thyself', and thought that I had just bought my neighbour.

Some days later, I was sitting on the balcony working at my notes when I heard shouting from the street. A dense column of Egyptians was approaching, and the purpose of their demonstration was heard in the anger of their multitudinous voice. Alone, some ten yards before the head of the column, was a young girl; every few yards she turned round to the marchers and flung her arms high into the air, shouting with all the passion of her being. I watched until the demonstration had passed. My uncle tapped me on the shoulder. 'Look at your cigarette,' he said. I had left it burning on the flat arm of a garden chair. 'You've ruined that chair,' he said.

I returned to England by way of Greece and Italy, and my father gave me £100 so that I would not have to touch my capital. At that time – May, 1921 – there were no tourists in Athens, and when I went to the Parthenon I was often alone, and became oppressed by the dead weight of time and the inability to do anything but look.

From Athens I went to Laurium, attracted by its position on the map on the very tip of the Attic peninsula. In the train, returning to their homes from the war with Turkey, were soldiers who looked like poor peasants in cast-off uniforms; and again I was conscious of being English, and through this aware-ness of my distance from them, I looked out at the olive groves on the bare and slowly passing hills.

From Laurium I walked to Sunium, where on a lonely head-land were the ruins of a temple and the only sound was the tinkle of a goat bell. I went to the edge of the cliff, saw the blue-green water below, climbed down and bathed naked. When I climbed to the top again, I thought I had not been sufficiently conscious that it was in that beautiful water that my body had floated, so I climbed down and went in again, but soon came out, disappointed. I asked for something to eat in a wayside house; and the woman having brought me the food, sat on a bench under a fly-blown oleograph of the King of Greece, with a coloured card stuck in the frame bearing the words 'Christ is Risen', and while she gave her baby the breast, she watched me.

I went on round the coast of the eastern Peloponnese, pleased with my wandering self-sufficiency. I got up early and bathed all morning, writing long letters in small handwriting to Paul, fairly regularly to my father and stepmother, sometimes to Constance. Now and then, after I had bathed, I wrote a poem. One began – and I thought it a good opening –

66

> Over the clear silence
> Left by the echo of the early hours
> The sky is poised in noon.
> Noon on the sea
> Dances in and out of nothing
> In an endless beginning.

I forget the rest of it, but it ended

> The sun
> Is the noon's superb will.

I tried to think that ending good also, but I knew that the
'superb will' was taken from Flaubert, and that I was not
speaking the phrase about the sun, but wished, beneath the
apparent impersonality, to heighten the impression of myself.
'Die Dichter lügen zu viel' – the poets lie too much – said
Zarathustra. My will was not superb. Sitting on the sand and
digging the spines of the sea-urchins out of my toes before going
to get some food, I thought that my reality is my body, not my
will, neither individualistic nor metaphysical; for I had known
that moment in the dining-hall in Trinity that my will was
nothing. I take no idea seriously, I thought; I try them on.

I went to the ancient Greek theatre of Epidaurus, sitting
beside a peasant in the front of his painted cart, watching the
rhythmically moving rump of his slow horse. He kept starting
to talk as if I could understand him; and when he gestured
with his whip, we stopped to drink wine at an inn beside the
dusty road. When we reached Epidaurus, I was heavy and lay
down under an olive tree and slept for nearly two hours. When
I woke, not fully refreshed, I went and sat down on the highest
tier of the empty amphitheatre and looked at the stage, where
tragedy had been acted, born out of the spirit of music. There
were wild flowers, growing out of every cranny between the
grey stones, and countless butterflies. We started back to Naup-
lion in the late afternoon. Girls returning from the fields called
to the driver, and he stopped, and they climbed in. Soon they
were all singing.

I got back in July, with presents for the family, and began
to work for an examination I should have to take to make up
for the year I had missed.

I went to see Thompson and Marie. Dancing with a girl at a party they had taken me to, I found we were dancing well together, as if our movement came from the dance itself. I took her out on the river and into the country, and we lay and kissed. But she said to me, 'You don't know the first thing about women'; then after three or four weeks, as I was seeing her home in a taxi, she said in a tone of amused regret, 'You have fallen out of love with me, this moment'. I also took out Nancy, whom I had met soon after my return from Ruhleben, and my stepmother was pleased. She said how nice I looked in the orange bow-tie I had taken to wearing occasionally. I replied that I thought it was a good thing to let myself go a bit, and she took my head in her arms and hugged it.

But she warned me that I must remember it was barely a year since I had had a bad haemorrhage. I owed it to my father not to make myself ill again, so I shouldn't go out so often in the evenings.

My brother Cecil, whom I had barely seen since the end of the war, also warned me that my father had his eye on me. In his tone there was still an echo of the old fear of provoking our father's anger. But with him that fear was only an unimportant survival, not an inhibiting power. He had never been so shut up within himself, but had understood that other people wanted to help him, and had gladly and gratefully taken their help. Mingled with our long brotherly affection and with the memory of the wonder I had felt for his daring when he was riding his bicycle and swung first one leg and then the other on to the handle-bars, there was respect for the purposefulness with which he devoted himself to his medical profession, and family admiration and pride that he had been decorated for tending the wounded under fire – even though in compensation I told myself that I was the more intelligent and sought opportunities to show it. But the affection and the respect were stronger than the envy; and when he warned me that my father was watching me, I knew that he wanted to help me. I didn't provoke a row.

For the first time in his life, my father, now on the threshold of old age, was building a house. We were acquainted with a professor of engineering at London University, brother of Cecil's professor of anatomy, who had designed a new cement block, eighteen inches by nine by nine for building. One block built as much wall as sixteen ordinary bricks, and being hollow and having an opening for the hand in one of its longer faces it could easily be handled by one man, and the air within would keep the temperature of the house equable. My father, who on the termination of his work at Woolwich Arsenal had been for a time an inspector for the Tottenham Gas Company, offered to build a house with these blocks to demonstrate they were all the professor claimed for them. Starting with a green field, my father in the early spring of this year, had set about building a six-roomed bungalow near Ruislip, with one and occasionally two labourers to help him.

I went down a few times with him. We rode on the 27 bus to Baker Street, going on top to smoke a cigarette, which, my father said, always lasted him to just beyond Mornington Crescent. I fetched and carried, and did any job that required neither skill nor much strength. We squatted on a plank and ate our sandwiches and handed to each other the bottle of beer, in the companionableness that came from working together; and even on my own tentative hands, now warm and dry instead of a little clammy, there was the good smell of the wheelbarrow. On the last day that we worked together, when there was already a hint of evening in the light and the shed had been locked up and we were about to go, my father stopped and looked at the low rising walls. He took me rather awkwardly by the arm, and said in his reflective voice, which I loved to hear, 'I never thought I should build a house'. Then he was silent, and I felt sure that he was thinking of himself and Mother, newly married, and of their son, me. I wanted to press his arm, but didn't. Then he repeated his favourite words from Ecclesiastes: 'Whatever thy hand findeth to do, do it with thy might'; and let go my arm.

In the autumn I went back to Dublin. I had decided to give up classics and to take my degree in French and German, and on the first day of lectures I took my place among the other students who had been following the course for three years. The French professor, who looked like a worldly abbot with his white-haired tonsured head and his benignly sensual face, asked me to what he owed the honour of my presence. I explained. 'You are confident that in one year you can master a four years honours course?' he asked. 'I think so,' I said. A girl sitting in the row in front of me turned round and looked at me. The professor noticed and smiled.

My stepmother had said that because of my lungs I should live outside Dublin (her sister had sold Ellerslie and moved to England). I got lodgings in a house on Howth headland, north of Dublin Bay. It was one of a row of detached five-room villas on the slope of a hill; and on the other side of the road, along which ran an hourly tram to connect with the train to Dublin, the ground fell sharply to the sea. The house belonged to a widow, Mrs Rudd, who had been a nurse, and her daughter, Ivy, lived with her.

When on the day of my arrival I was finishing beside the fire the tea which Mrs Rudd had given me, her daughter returned home from the office in Dublin where she worked as a typist. I heard from the little hall a friendly voice calling 'Mother!', and Mrs Rudd telling her, 'He's in the front room', and then she came in. She was dressed in a fur-trimmed dark mauve costume which matched her eyes, and when she took off her hat with a free movement of her arm and a twist of her neck there was a mass of fine light golden hair piled high on the top of her head. She sat down and we chatted, and I saw that she had hardly any chin.

Mother and daughter looked after me. As at home, I had a glass of milk at night, and there was now a hot-water-bottle in my bed; and at the end of the week Mrs Rudd urged me, as my stepmother would have done, to get out and eat the air. Five days a week I went into College, taking the same tram as Ivy, who was never ready till the last moment, so that we often had to race down the zig-zagging path; and as we sat down side by side in the moving tram, she laughed breathlessly.

Besides the work for the university course I also wrote sketches about Egypt and Greece, which were published in the *Manchester Guardian* and the *Irish Times*. Seeing it in print, I felt that the 'I' at the centre of the world so carefully described was not myself. There was more, I thought, in a paper I read to the University Philosophical Society, which I entitled *The Need of a New Myth*. All the old myths, I said, were dead. The pyramids and sphinxes of Egypt, the mummified bulls, dogs and cats, the riot of gods and goddesses with the heads of cows, jackals and apes, were incomprehensible. Apollo and Dionysus had gone and only stones remained. Where there had been the Christian soul, now there was the unconscious. Know thyself, the Delphic oracle had said; but the terms of that knowledge today did not make possible any active living. There could only be the will to assert the myth of ourselves. But remembering what I had thought about my will after writing the poem about the sun, this also seemed to be a kind of showing off.

In Mrs Rudd's front room there was a piano, on which, after I had finished working, Ivy strummed dance tunes and accompanied herself as she sang *Margie* and *Whisper that you will never leave me;* and after two or three weeks I was joining in. When Ivy and her mother had gone up to bed, I sat in the big armchair beside the fire with the words running in my head

> Whisper that you will not deceive me,
> Whisper that you will never leave me,
> Whisper that you love but me.

We are going to have a love affair, I said to myself, and this song is its mythology.

I thought that I ought not to let the love affair begin; and to strengthen that resolve I wrote long letters to Paul, now in Berlin as agent for his brother, with critical summaries of the lectures on Gautier and Baudelaire and enclosing the travel sketches that had been published. But as I put the letter in the envelope, I knew that I would go on.

We walked on the headland in the wind and the sun, her eyes the same colour as where the shadow of a cloud lay on the sea. When I helped with the washing-up after supper, Ivy and her mother teased me because my movements were clumsy and excused me because I was a scholar. I took Ivy to a dance, and as we returned home by the last train, I looked at her lying back in the corner of our empty compartment, holding her fur coat loosely around her, and my heart pounded. One Sunday evening in November we had been sitting side by side in two arm-chairs before the fire, and placing our elbows on the arm of my chair we had been forcing back each other's wrists. Then Ivy said she must go and help get supper. I said

I would come and lay the table, but Ivy said 'No', and stood with her back to the door and her palms pressed against it, laughing. I put my arms under her shoulders to pull her away; and without knowing I was going to do so, I kissed her. She looked at me, in eager surprise. 'It isn't you,' she said. I looked back at her, and heard my voice saying, 'Ivy, I warn you. Whatever I say, don't believe me.'

In the evenings, when Mrs Rudd had gone up, Ivy stayed with me for half-an-hour or more, and we sat in the armchair and kissed. She told me that she had been engaged and that her fiancé had been killed in the war. 'They were very fond of us,' she said, which I thought a curious use of the plural, 'but not like you'. Then I heard her moving about overhead as she went to bed, and her mother's voice talking to her, and I wondered what they were saying, as I sat on in the comfortable room, consciously deceiving them until there would be an unimaginable end. My passivity, I thought, has in it a desire of destruction, and perhaps that is the evil power I felt beneath my quietness when I was writing the note on Nietzsche's aphorism.

Paul wrote that he had to go to Vienna and asked me to join him there for Christmas. 'Will you tell your friend about me?' Ivy asked on the evening before I left. 'No,' I answered. Paul, however, guessed, and told me not to take it so seriously and not to do anything stupid. He talked of the women and writers and business men he met in Berlin, and how he had now freed himself from the romantic clichés of 'the eternities and the immensities'. I had never been, he said, so romantic as he, and as I started off without that handicap my travel sketches were very nicely written. 'But what,' he asked, 'are you trying to say?' I remembered what he had said about my poems, and couldn't answer. As my train drew out of the station, and I raised the window again after waving to him and went back to my seat, I felt without hope.

I told Ivy that we must stop, but in a few days we began again. 'You're not playing with her?' Mrs Rudd asked. 'No,' I answered. We became engaged. 'She won't come to you with nothing,' Mrs Rudd said, 'because she'll have the house when I'm gone.' 'I've got a little of my own that my mother left me,' I said. 'It's not much, is it?' Mrs Rudd asked. 'Just enough for me to live on.' 'Oh,' Mrs Rudd said, and looked at me closely. 'Well,' she said, after a short pause, 'that'll be a nice little bit extra.'

I gave Ivy an ivory necklace, but not a ring; she gave me a silver match-box that held a photograph of herself – full face, I observed, because her profile was bad.

It was understood that we could not think of marrying till I had my degree, which would be in October. So I had time. I thought that between then and now my lungs might get bad again; but since that was uncertain, I began to think of suicide.

January and February went by. Paul wrote to me, but I didn't answer. At last I said one morning that I should be back late from a meeting of the Philosophical Society, and returning at night I went down to the seashore, and sitting on a rock cut at my left wrist with a safety razor blade I had brought with me till the blood began to flow freely, though I was not at all sure that I had severed the vein. Then, going into the sea in all my clothes and overcoat, I lay down in a crevice among the rocks like a sarcophagus, with some idea that the rising tide would drown me, though I didn't know whether the tide was rising or not. It was a calm night, and the water slopped gently over the rocks, while my hat floated like a dark drunken boat a few feet out. Now and again the water heaved and lifted my body and then let it down again, and a pointed rock caught me in the small of my back, and I shifted to lie more comfortably. From time to time I lifted up my wrist, and the blood was still flowing. My life being finished, I thought that in my last moments I should see the truth; but no revelation came. The water heaved and fell and lifted in the calm night as if I wasn't there.

I lay there about a quarter of an hour. Then I said aloud, 'This is bloody ridiculous'. I got to my feet and retrieved my hat. I explained to Mrs Rudd – Ivy was in bed – that as it was such a fine night I had come back by the cliff path and had stumbled in the darkness and fallen into the sea and cut myself on a sharp rock. She made me take a hot bath and drink a large glass of hot milk and brandy against pneumonia; and I went to bed and slept soundly.

Next day the despondency returned. Mrs Rudd's mention of

pneumonia made me think I could provoke it; so the following morning I soaked my woollen vest in cold water before I put it on.

I did that for several mornings, but I never even sneezed. I had read a novel by the Swiss writer Carl Spitteler, entitled *Imago*, whose hero, a writer, used to call his body 'Konrad', and when he woke from a refreshing sleep, he would say, 'Thank you, Konrad'. My Konrad, I thought, must have taken me pretty effectively in his charge; and as I thought it, I knew that soon I would say that I couldn't marry Ivy.

I did say it, after two or three days during which Mrs Rudd said I had become a black stranger. I told her first, and she said she would tell Ivy, who was in bed with a cold. Mrs Rudd came down after a few minutes, and said to me, 'You can go up now'.

Ivy was leaning against the pillows, her eyes filled with tears. 'It's funny, isn't it,' she said, 'I thought from the beginning that you were a fraud – no, not a fraud, but not genuine.'

'I've told her,' I said to Mrs Rudd when I went downstairs. She took me by the wrist and shook it gently up and down. 'You're fickle,' she said, 'and I'm very sorry for you. You're self-centred because you think you can afford to be. That's the truth about you, Alick. Remember.'

I remembered, but didn't think about it.

Glad to be alive and free, I very soon forgot Ivy. I went to live in Dublin and had a love-affair with Doris, the girl who had turned round to look at me on the first day of lectures. Of the fighting in Dublin that summer I heard the gunfire.

CHAPTER VI

I got my degree in October, 1922, but had no thought of making a career. I went to a small village above the Rhone valley in Switzerland as tutor to a boy whose father was the poorly paid editor of a magazine for English residents abroad, and my salary just covered board and lodging in a 'family hotel'.

My room was small, with a creaking wardrobe and brown linoleum. In the evenings there was nowhere else to sit except a lounge with wicker chairs, an upright piano and a palm tree beside it on a tall green stand. The season had not yet begun and the hotel was half empty. After the first few days I had become acquainted with the other residents: an ageing, heavy French girl, who used to play *J'en ai marre* and *Coal Black Mammy*, a retired Swiss schoolmaster, and two English spinsters, one of whom used regularly to play, as if it were a waltz, the first movement of the Moonlight Sonata.

There was also an English woman, whom I judged to be about five years older than I, with her son, aged seven, whom she had brought into the mountains because she was concerned about his health. He had my Christian names – John Alexander; and was called Johnnie. Her name was Katherine Gordon. She had a lovely broad and open brow; sensitive, humorous and steady eyes; and there was a sad curve on her lips, which made me think of a young bird.

Her husband was with her on a short visit. He was a high official in the civil service, with an unassuming authority in his manner and a boyish, toothy grin. He was determinedly on holiday and joined heartily in the singing of *Coal Black Mammy*. He was interested that I had been in Egypt, and talked about the political and economic condition of the country with clarity and knowledge. He asked me what I was going to be and I answered easily that I might later get a post as lecturer.

I liked the boy, Bobbie, whom I had to teach, and fortunately he took to me. Whatever awe he may have felt of me as his 'tutor', he lost when he discovered the gaps in my know-

75

ledge of mathematics, for which he was gifted. I had to teach him mornings and afternoons, with alternate Saturdays off. In the evenings I often wrote to Doris and suggested that we should meet for Christmas; and also to Paul, in order to assure myself that I hadn't joined the people in the lounge. One evening, as I was writing in my room, I heard the sound of a Chopin prelude, and when I went down it was Katherine Gordon playing.

Early in December the snow came, and I went ski-ing with Bobbie. I soon learned to stay on my feet, and sometimes went off alone to the higher slopes. Often the whole valley was filled with a sea of cloud, out of which rose the sunlit mountains, and the silence of the bright dunes of snow around me was like the desert. Once I heard the distant throbbing; as it ceased, the sunlit stillness seemed the form of time, and again there was that wonder which the mind could not grasp that there should be anything.

Johnnie wanted to ski, so I took him out sometimes to an easy slope in front of the hotel, while his mother, wrapped in a fur-coat almost as dark as her hair, sat and watched us. It became the habit that I should come and say goodnight to him, tell him stories and play to him on his mouth-organ, while his mother moved about the room.

Doris had written to say that she didn't think it would be right for her to come away at Christmas, and my letters to her began to be less frequent. Early in the next year, 1923, I left the hotel and took a room with a big balcony in an isolated chalet outside the village.

I hired a piano, and Mrs Gordon came to tea and played to me. The chalet where I had my room belonged to an old, shrewd countrywoman, Madame Kehrli, who had rarely been out of the village. I asked her if Mrs Gordon might come and practise on the piano while I was out at work. She answered kindly, 'Let her come, young man'. She did come sometimes in the mornings when Johnnie was having his lessons with his French governess; and Madame Kehrli brought her coffee, and they liked each other. I read to Katherine – for we now called each other by our Christian names – some of my poems, and I gave her Graeme's book.

Sometimes Johnnie came with her; and so that there might

be less talk, I sometimes asked the English spinsters, and the retired schoolmaster, to supper.

When the winter was coming to an end, Katherine and I became lovers. As the days grew warmer, we sometimes lay on the balcony in the sunlight, and were very happy. There was hardly a house to be seen, only the fields disappearing into the valley, as at the lip of a waterfall, and a great open sky curving to meet the distant mountains on the further side. I would go and make the supper, and afterwards Katherine would play, and was happy when I once said to her, 'This is almost the nicest part of the evening'.

In the summer we managed to have a week-end on a remote lake, and found a quiet bay where we could bathe naked. Katherine was as happy as a child. Standing on the firm, sandy bottom, the water just coming to the top of her thighs, she kept rising on her toes and with her cupped hands sending drops of water high into the air; and as the sun was behind her, they sparkled with light against the sky. In the night I dreamt I was giving her a drink of water from a silver cup; and waking up, I got out of bed and brought her a glass. 'How did you know?' she said: 'I was afraid to wake you.' She drank and went peacefully to sleep, with her head on my breast.

We knew it couldn't last beyond the summer, when she must go back to England and to her husband. She hated deceit, so she had told him of our relationship, and he said she could do what she liked, so long as it was in a small resort in Switzerland and there was no scandal. She also told one of her friends, a Lady X, who came to visit her for a few days. She was considerably older than Katherine, ugly and intelligent; and I felt that between them there was complete trust. She invited me to dinner with her and Katherine at the Grand Palais Hotel, and Katherine told me not to be nervous: 'She knows about us'. As we were drinking sherry in the lounge and I was watching the people while she and Katherine were talking, she unexpectedly laid her bony hand over mine, and with a little pat and a most friendly smile, she said, 'You dear socialist, you're hating us all, aren't you?' I was surprised and interested, for it hadn't occurred to me that I might be a socialist. Then Katherine also patted my hand, and said, 'He's not a socialist. He's only detached, because he's a poet'.

Her voice seemed to give the word a capital letter, and I was uncomfortable. Her intonations, I sometimes said to myself, put me on the top of the Alps. For though her voice was gentle, it sometimes imitated the constricted social tone.

When I noticed it, all my dissatisfaction with myself returned. I wrote out some of the stories I told Johnnie – A man felt his worries and cares so much that he went out to lose them under the open sky, and saw a duck in a pond, and liking the way it looked at him out of one eye he took it home and kept it in the bath – and thought they were quite pleasant; and I also wrote some poems. But I wasn't working; I was acquiescing, I told myself, in what I didn't believe in. I made cutting remarks to Katherine about the English spinsters and about Philistine respectability; and I told her she wasn't serious enough about her music.

Once we quarrelled about Johnnie. I said that the hotel was a bad environment for him, that his governess was stupid, and that sometimes his eyes were very unhappy. Katherine turned on me. 'How dare you say my Johnnie is unhappy?'

When her anger had passed a little, she said – and she said it at other times also – that I was always looking for something wrong in other people because I didn't like myself. 'Why can't you take other people,' she asked, 'as they are? And yourself.' I'll be damned if I will, I thought. I quoted Nietzsche to her, 'Become what you are'; to say that one should take people as they are was a lazy, complacent denial of what they could and should become and an excuse for relaxing in what Nietzsche called 'miserable comfort'. 'But you tell them to be what they can't be,' Katherine said, 'and when they can't you feel self-righteous. You tell me to work harder at the piano, but you know as well as I do that I'm not a musician. I'm a woman, and you have no idea what scenes I spare you. You want to make me different, as if you demeaned yourself by loving me as I am. You're afraid to admit that you need to love.'

I knew I had hurt her, and was sorry. I cowered at what she said about me, and then put it from me.

Before Katherine went back to England, we had three days on one of the Italian lakes; twenty-four hours more; still the night. The train entered the Simplon tunnel, and the wall flickered and roared past our window. I said to Katherine, 'It's like dying', and she nodded wordlessly. Then the noise changed its key, and we were out in the daylight.

At Brig we said goodbye on the platform. When her train had gone, I went out into the small town, whose indifference I could neither endure nor resist.

We met again in London in the late summer. I took a room in Paddington, the family being away in France, and Katherine came when she could get away. I was invited to dinner at their house and then to the theatre to see Yvonne Arnaud in *Tons of Money*. Her husband promoted me, as being his wife's lover, from 'West', as he had called me when we sang *Coal Black Mammy*, to 'Mr West'. Katherine told me in a quick, low voice that he wasn't going away after all to a conference which would have given her several days of freedom. As we held hands in the dark of the theatre, in her tight clasp I felt her unhappiness.

I asked her to leave her husband. I could find work in Dublin, and to tide us over I had £200, paid to me as compensation for injury to health due to internment. Katherine said she could never leave Johnnie; but then she asked, 'If I don't come to you, would it mean that I could never see you again?' 'No,' I replied, and thought as I said it, that she wanted me to say 'Yes', and so make her come.

In early September my father and stepmother returned from France and I went home to Highgate. 'Now what?' said my father in a friendly tone. He suggested I should work for a Ph.D. degree so that I should be better qualified for a university post. I could agree, I thought, and say to my father that I would take the degree in German literature and would have to do a year's research at the university in Berlin, where Paul was pressing me to join him. Until the year was up, I needn't say that I wouldn't take the degree. So I had an interview with a professor at Cambridge, who urged me to write on the German influences in the work of the Irish poet, Mangan. 'Think,' he said, in a tone almost of ecstasy. 'Future scholars will go to their shelves and say "Here is West on Mangan".' There would be no West on Mangan, but it would sound all right at home.

But until the beginning of the university term I put off going to Berlin. While I delayed, I read in a German translation

79

Dostoevsky's *A Raw Youth,* and one sentence made an impression of which I told nobody: Das Gute, das Du zu tun gedenkst, tu' es nicht aus Neid, sondern um Gottes willen – the good that you mean to do, do not do it out of envy, but for the sake of God. I remembered what Katherine had said to me about my refusal to admit my need to love. The motive strongest in me, I thought, is envy. I envy Paul because he is free. I try to imitate him and believe that I also am myself. But David said that I won't let myself be what I am. Then I imagined myself doing good, not out of envy, but for the sake of God, and I was surprised by joy.

The train was nearing Berlin, and I looked continuously out of the left-hand window. On that side would be Ruhleben. For a moment I saw the low red barracks, the flagstaff and the sandy compound, now green. Then they were gone.

Paul was no longer working for his brother, but doing commercial translations and giving English lessons to bankers and to the staff of big firms, like the A.E.G.. In a well-appointed flat near the Kurfürstendamm, in the West End of Berlin, he had a spacious room, with a large bedroom opening off it. As you came in, you would involuntarily stop and look round at the pictures which Paul had bought in the inflation – an Ascent of Christ, possibly by Le Sueur, as Paul only half seriously told visitors, a Spanish shepherd with his flute, an early German landscape, an Adam and Eve holding hands beneath the Tree of Life, the apple still on the bough; and you would be aware of the maroon-coloured strip of Japanese embroidered silk on the top of the open piano, and the Hiroshige print, with the deep blue, on the wall above it; and on the small tables and low bookcases there were Roman and Greek heads, Tang horses, inros and netsukes – words which I now heard for the first time.

Living with him was Jeanne, half-French, half-English, a few years younger than I. She had straight, black shining hair, drawn back from a beautiful forehead, high and strong cheekbones, eyes like pools in a peat stream; and the contentment on her gently closed lips was like the beginning of a smile. We had already met in Thompson's flat in London, and we liked each other. Later she told me that she had been more strongly attracted to me physically than to any man she had met. 'But now it's gone', she said. She could lie by the hour on the divan, sleeping like a cat, while Paul played the piano; and she seemed to have no thought of time. She was supposed to be studying dancing; but her dancing was like my Ph.D. degree.

She was cool and self-sufficient, and she seemed to me not so much to love Paul, whom she used to call smilingly 'Mr Pan', as to enjoy his being; and she and I were united in the knowledge that he was greater than either of us. For he had that peculiar power of penetrating beneath the social manner which people assumed to the desires and fears, conscious and unconscious, which made them assume it. When Jeanne and I were alone together, I felt as if nothing was happening and I had neither the power nor the wish to make anything happen; but as soon as Paul came in and started to talk, there was life. Because in them, as he often said, there was life and freedom, he had the pictures in his room and the carvings and vases. Also when he had been playing the piano, he would say, 'I'm getting more free'; and he would shake out his small, old-looking hands.

He was glad that I was with him, and by his manner constantly told me that I had done right to leave home and come to Berlin, and that I could now make myself a writer. But his encouragement, as if in spite of himself, was qualified. 'You can always hope to do good work,' he once said to me. 'You'll have hope for a good fifteen years yet.' That would take me to forty-four, I thought; and I was struck by his casual frankness. Was that his real opinion of me, that there wasn't enough to last over middle age?

After I had been in Berlin a couple of months, Paul said to me, 'You are still only half here'. As usual, when he spoke to me about myself, I felt that he was telling me the truth. My not being at home was as real to me as my being in Berlin. I wrote almost every day to Katherine, and when Paul asked me if I felt myself pledged to be faithful to her, I said that I did.

I felt also that I withdrew from him into my writing. I came over to his flat for breakfast – I had a room about a quarter of a mile away – and in the morning I used to work at a desk by the window. Often Paul or Jeanne would be playing the piano, but in Ruhleben I had got used to noise and it didn't worry me.

I wrote some poems and began a novel about myself and Lotte in the village on the Baltic coast before the war. As I had been reading Proust, I thought I would get on the track of my own *temps perdu*, and began to write out a list of memories. I tried phantasmagoria about suppressed complexes, and the ancestral inhabitants of the Id overpowering the Super-ego and sending out the self-observing prig in whom they had to live on a glorious night of riot and lechery. I kept notes of my numberless dreams, and wrote some of them up into fantasies: a boy set out to chase the sun, but when he had crossed three fields the sun said to him that he must say 'A-Philip, B-Philip, C-Philip' to the end of the alphabet, and the boy stuttered and had to stand still, and the sun went on his way. Jeanne liked all that I wrote, and Paul said that the novel had a pleasant personal quality, but by occasional remarks about the poems and the fantasies I felt him telling me that with passive obstinacy I was refusing to come out of myself.

He urged me to read Spengler's *Decline of the West,* and I did so. I disliked Spengler's arrogance, but thought he had some right to it. Scholars and professors, he said, collected facts, but were mentally so inert that they never even thought of examining the conceptions by which they ordered the facts. They divided history into 'antiquity', 'the middle ages', and 'modern times', as if there were no history but what had begun in their 'antiquity', and their 'modern times' merely went on. In reality, history was a succession of cultures, whose only meaning was their growth, flowering and dying. The spirit of our Western culture was the desire of Faust for the unattainable, the urge towards the horizon, our sense of time and history. In this last period of decline, when our culture had already created its expressive forms and, like a plant, having flowered once could flower no more, the only cultural activity still possible to us was to be conscious of the inevitability of our own decay.

It pleased me that in the paper I had read at Trinity I also had said that all previous forms of knowledge had lost their meaning; and I thought that what I had called the need of a new myth would perhaps be satisfied if we made the consciousness of approaching death into our form of life. But my actual response to Spengler was not an awareness of Western culture's inevitable decay, but a new sense that I participated in its being. Once I was walking along the Spree and a swan moved across the still reflections in the water. Trees and buildings and sky were broken into rippling fragments, and I stayed to watch until they had resumed their unreal being. I thought that I did not watch only because I was myself, but because I belonged to Western culture which loved time and change, and that my pleasure in watching was because I shared that love.

Paul then formed a theory of his own. Commenting on one of my childhood memories, he had said that there were two kinds of activity: there were actions you could do whenever you wanted since you needed only yourself to do them, like running or singing; and there were actions for which, like the child at the breast, you needed another person. The first kind of action he called individual activity; and the second, group activity. Then he said this was true also of cultures. Spengler, however, had wrongly taken Faust as representative of the whole of Western culture; but Faust was its hero only in its period of individual activity. Prior to this, there had been the period of group activity. From the birth of our culture in Christianity before the time of Charlemagne until the close of the middle ages, the group had been supreme, and the individual had existed only as part of the whole. This unity was maintained by the Catholic Church: it was formulated in its theology, made visible in the cathedral, lived by the people in the celebration of the Mass. Then the organic unity gave way to individualism and tragedy was born. But the individual was unable to bear alone the tragic consciousness of transience and death; the strong individualism of Descartes – *I* think, therefore *I* am – became the weak individualism of romanticism. Individuals now needed each other's support, but organic unity was gone and today no unity was possible except the artificial unity of association, as in a political party or a trade union. These, Paul said, were the three periods of our culture: the unity of the organic group; individualism; collective association. In each period, the experience and the conception of reality, and – since no reality existed except as conceived – reality itself, were fundamentally different. In the phrase which Paul came to use more and more often, there were 'three realities'.

He asked me my opinion, and I said that there was something in the idea. He spoke of it continually and with growing excitement, and I felt him pressing me to accept it. One evening when I had been sitting quiet at the supper table, Jeanne – she had been reading my description of how I had felt a little man inside me, watching, when my father had told us of our mother's death – said to me, half teasing, half affectionate, 'What's the little man doing?'; and as I smiled at her, Paul said, 'Growing up, eh, old son?' Both of us knew what he meant: that I should cease to be pre-occupied with myself and should help him work out his theory of 'the three realities'. And I knew that I never would.

Then he would make me play with him a Haydn symphony arranged for four hands on the piano, and the music filled me with pleasure and with friendliness towards him. 'He is greater than I am,' I thought, 'and what can I do better than help him?'

In the late summer of 1924 Cecil was to be married, and the wedding was to be in Dublin. Katherine wrote to me that she could get away for a week, and we arranged to meet before I crossed to Ireland.

Since Jeanne had decided that she would study dancing in London, Paul asked me to take her over with me. At Dover, as I waited for her to come out of the Aliens Department, a policeman came up and said, 'The Immigration Officer wants to see you'. I was shown into a small office. 'How much of this young lady's money have you got?' a smooth-voiced official asked me. 'Not much,' I stammered. 'Have you any?' 'About £2.' 'How is she going to live?' And then: 'Where did you meet her? What do you do in Berlin? Who is Mr Paul Farleigh? With what teacher is this girl going to study dancing?' And then: 'Why don't you admit that she is your mistress?' 'Because she's not.' Then: 'Where are you going? Is this friend you are going to meet a man or a woman? What is her name?' 'She is a married woman and I refuse to tell you.' 'We shall find out.' More questions, and at last: 'In Dover we know the secrets of men's hearts.' 'You don't know mine,' I said.

Jeanne was not allowed to land. I went up to London and cashed a cheque, so that she would have money. When I saw her on the steamer, calm and grateful, she said that she would go to Paris, where she had friends. Then I went to meet Katherine, the fury not yet subsided.

According to the supposed plan, I should now, the year's research at Berlin University being over, go to Cambridge. When the wedding was over and we were back in Highgate, I told my father as we were going a walk over Parliament Fields, that I wasn't going to take the Ph.D. degree, and that I would go back to Berlin. He tried, without anger, to dissuade me, telling me that I was spoiling my life. But at last he said that he supposed I must do what I felt I ought to do. 'Only be sure you do it,' he said.

Before leaving England a week or so later, I went with Katherine to an exhibition of Gauguin's works, and then twice by myself, since I was deeply moved. I was held by an early self-portrait, in which he seemed to be looking out of a small prison window; and the painting of Jacob wrestling with the Angel, watched by a ring of peasant faces in white coifs, on a background like that before your eyes when you shut them and look at the sun, recalled how I had been moved as a child by the reading of the story in the Bible and by Jacob's words, 'I will not let thee go unless thou tell thy name to me'.

I got all the books on Gauguin I could find, with reproductions of his paintings, and when I was back in Berlin I started to write about him. It became a short book, but during the war the manuscript was lost, and I can't remember what I said. But I know that I often looked at the orange background in the picture of Jacob wrestling with the Angel. In that light beyond my eyelids and in the darkness before sleep, I was seeing what I most wanted to know. I was also held by the woodcuts in *Noa-Noa,* and I used to look first at the picture of the imprisoned self and then at their darkness and freedom and sexual forms; and it was this liberation which I tried to understand and describe. Paul said that I had read myself into the pictures; and though I thought that what I had found in them might still be true, I was unsatisfied.

In the late summer of 1925 Paul went home to see his father and mother. I took over some of his pupils, one of them a woman I had seen for a few moments when she came for her lessons, and to whom I was strongly attracted. On the first afternoon, we looked at each other and kissed. The next

85

couple of weeks we spent all the time we could together, going dancing till the early hours; and I didn't write to Katherine.

Then one morning I woke up and coughed, and again there was blood in my mouth.

CHAPTER VII

I went to see a doctor, bearded and stern, who told me to creep up the stairs lest I should bring on another haemorrhage, and demonstrated how I should blow my nose, one nostril at a time, so as not to compress the air. 'So soll der Mensch sich schnaufen,' he said – That is how man should blow his nose.

I went home, and it was decided that I must go to a sanatorium in Switzerland. The specialist who examined me said, 'You must have great powers of resistance'. Remembering Konrad and his frustration of my attempts to give myself pneumonia, I thought they were greater than he knew.

Before I left England, I had to have all my teeth out because of pyorrhoea. When I came out of the darkness of the gas, in which I had been crushed by some enormous question, and leaned forward to rinse out my mouth, strewn over the floor round the dentist's chair I saw my teeth with their bloody fanged roots. 'You're having a bad time, my poor lad,' my father said, as he took my arm firmly in his and led me home. We passed a poster on a hoarding: 'Extraction of the teeth is no cure for pyorrhoea'; and I thought that often what happened to me was slightly comic.

From Paris I travelled by the night train, third-class. The only other occupant of the compartment was a girl with a humorous intelligent face, who, as she told me later, was starting work in a hotel in Alsace. Toothless, I nevertheless said to myself, 'I will kiss you before the night is over'. And when in the small hours I had settled back in my corner again and we were drinking from the bottle of wine I had brought, she said, with a tone of friendly knowledge of what men are like, 'Do you feel better now?'

The train climbed and the mountains closed in. Then we entered a curving tunnel and emerged into the bottom of a hole shut in by a mountain so high and near that by the early afternoon the sun was gone. The sanatorium was a cold rectangle, with wide, echoing staircases. But the spacious dining-room, and the five-course dinner, were as in a first-class hotel. There was, however, little sound of conversation; and a woman at a nearby table, with a book propped up against a water-jug, made me think of Keats's line: 'And there I sat and read like a picture of somebody reading'. 'Do you know what this place is?' an Englishman already in his second year said to me over our coffee in the lounge. 'Prison with French cooking.' An electric bell rang, loud and persistent as a burglar alarm. '*Liegekur,*' he explained. 'All good patients out on the balcony.'

I was indeed reminded of internment. Our sanatorium was cut off from the world as we in Ruhleben had been, not by war, but by the authority of the doctors and by the morbid activity each of us carried within him. Without work we were housed and fed, and the bill which lay by my plate every Saturday morning was discharged by drawing on the account opened for me by my father at the bank in the village. Towards the other inmates I felt an obscure resentment and jealousy, as if the blustering, bandy-legged cavalry captain and the limp Oxford undergraduate nicknamed 'Concave Charlie', had no right to my disease.

When I went to lie out on the balcony, I took Spengler, Freud and La Rochefoucauld, and a pad to make notes and write letters to Paul. On one side of me was a young Chinaman with a collapsed lung, whom I liked, though we rarely talked. He used to read aloud to himself in a low muttering voice and suddenly go off in fits of inexplicable laughter; and he loved to say, when the white-coated doctor came round, 'Ah wanna be blawn up.' On the other side was a German school-teacher, fat and with superfluous hair, who practised her English by talking to me about Spengler and with more serious interest about possible reasons why her thermometer, which she kept in her mouth even beyond the prescribed ten minutes, registered a few points higher or lower than on the previous day. I read of patients who, when fire broke out in their sanatorium, rescued only their thermometers and temperature charts; and determining not to be like them, I marked up my chart without taking my temperature, as I knew I had no fever.

I began to read Thomas Mann's *Der Zauberberg,* but out of a healthy instinct, as I told myself, soon stopped. I felt that the book untruly interpreted illness and time and made them, equally and indifferently, the essence of being; but I wanted to keep my own being free so that I should not be united with the

Philistines in the general rivalry of being more interestingly ill.

But my mind came back to my illness. I read and wrote about five or six hours a day; but whether I read or wrote or thought, I felt that I had no firm bearings. I recalled some story of a man lost in the catacombs; and when his body was found, the soles of his shoes were worn through. Though I was not frightened, I felt that fear was not far off. I could not escape, I told myself, from the perpetual tension between myself and reality. The mountain was before me, in being from moment to moment, like a silent sound; and I, lying in the Liegehalle with the people around me, all of us wrapped and laid out – this also was unalterable. Why did I watch the mountain, in the inexorably moving sunlight that revealed its form against the blue sky, under dull cloud, through the falling snow, beneath the small moon? Because of Spengler's Faustian urge that drove us to the rim of the world. Because I was living, as Paul said, in the period of weak individualism and must identify myself with the mountain in order to feel that I too could stand alone. Because its rounded mass was a Freudian symbol of the mother's breast, and as I followed its line I was being lived by my Oedipus complex. Because the mountain was a Jungian archetype, and in the collective darkness within me was ancestral memory. Recalling La Rochefoucauld, I thought my motive was the envious wish to appear profound. 'The good that you mean to do, do not do it out of envy': what good did I mean to do?

Perhaps I might hold within my mind all my conflict and in my writing show the power of consciousness to be itself and to shine in its own chaos. But I was no such genius. Then I thought of the cavity in my lungs, and the freedom of death ravaging in the darkness, and I wished I could draw all the world into myself, and devour and destroy God. Then I thought of the witches' sabbath and the Black Mass, and tried to do automatic writing.

The hours when I read and wrote were few among the hours and hours of getting up, having meals, strolling about, going into the village to buy cigarettes and drink coffee in the Kursaal, talking to the woman I had noticed self-consciously reading on the first evening – a Frau Professor Heinz from Zürich. I wasn't lost in catacombs, I thought. I was punctual for meals. With my toothless gums I could manage everything except grapes. I had overcome my embarrassment and tried to talk well to Frau Professor Heinz and her courteous American friend. Whatever I think about Spengler and Freud, this is what I do: I lead a social life. Three cultured people, as my stepmother would call us, retire from the lounge which the cavalry captain's set have made their club, and in a small music-room we spend an agreeable evening and cut our *Liegekur*. Frau Professor Heinz and her friend do not hide, and I accept, their relationship of former lovers. There is a pleasant feeling between us, and we make pleasant conversation about culture and psychoanalysis; and I exploit Paul's idea of 'the three realities'. We pursue no question to the end, lest it should become tedious and heavy. We talk, I thought, out of *amour propre* and social considerateness; we confirm for each other our superiority to the set in the lounge.

Then it struck me, as it had not done before, that I was no better than they; for when I was alone, I was no more serious about my ideas. I read Freud and thought about my unconscious, but only in general terms. I decided to analyze my dreams and to try to form a theory about myself.

The theory I reached was that my mother had been for me the object of sexual interest as shown by a memory of sitting on the dresser while I put my foot into the shoe she was holding. I remembered her coming out with me to see the eclipse of the sun because I wanted the father, not the son, to be eclipsed. When she went away to Heaven, I bore resentment against her. The 'little man' within me who had wondered whether I would cry was this resentful and repressed ego, who, being abandoned to himself, would not join in my father's and brothers' sorrow. I had then introjected my mother into myself in order to possess her by being her, and had consequently adopted a feminine attitude towards my father. I had therefore not wanted to grow up because I didn't wish my child's body to become masculine, and I had never become a proper man. I had never overcome my fear of my father, nor of his substitute images, Thompson and Paul. Therefore I thought of committing suicide rather than marry Ivy: I could not marry because I was for myself a woman and didn't dare to become a husband and a father.

90

But then I thought of Konrad and how I had not once sneezed though morning after morning I put on a vest soaked in cold water. And just as, when reading, I would feel with certainty that here is something unresolved whose meaning is to be discovered, so I felt attracted by the peculiar and slightly comic contrast between the image of my feminine, fearful, perpetual pre-puberty self, whom I supposed to be the small reality within me, and my outward self in activity; and I remembered the humour in the girl's tone and look as she said to me, 'Do you feel better now?'

Then I told myself that unconscious resistance had sent Konrad into my mind, and that this was proof of my not having reached the roots. I continued to search for the meaning of an image from a dream.

The dream was that near the edge of a pavement, whose kerb was about a foot high, there stood a milestone, and close to it there were two stone steps up to the pavement from the roadway. Nothing happened. At first, I was sure that the milestone was on North Hill, Highgate, which ran down at the back of our house in Talbot Road. Then I remembered Dick Whittington's Stone, standing within railings, at the foot of Highgate Hill, and I was no longer sure. Then the milestone reminded me of the small dome which I used to see on the top of locomotive boilers half-way between the funnel and the driver's cabin; and I was persuaded beyond doubt that somewhere in Highgate there was such an iron dome standing half-buried in the pavement. But where? Now I have it: it was the boundary stone set in the russet-brick wall surrounding the graveyard of Highgate School Chapel, where between the railings you could see the sunken gravestones. No, it was somewhere in Parliament Fields; no, I was confusing it with the dome of St. Paul's which you could see from the top of Parliament Hill; no, I was confusing it with what was called Boadicea's Grave, a clump of old thick hawthorn trees, also surrounded by railings, on the top of a rise. Clearly, the stone was a symbol of the mother, and the railings around it were a father symbol. Why, though I recognized their unconscious significance, was I under this compulsion to identify the milestone and the iron dome? Where had I seen them? Or had I never seen them?

I turned to the steps beside the stone. I recalled immediately the passage from *Also Sprach Zarathustra*: 'You have jumped a step, and that is what no step forgives you'; and David saying 'You won't let yourself be what you are'. When I left David for the Arts and Science Union, I jumped what I am.

It was vanity that had made me jump the step. I had dropped David in order to be Hilda Wangel – an artificial woman applauded by imprisoned men.

Then I imagined the step I had jumped as not being there: the darkness into which I penetrated when I made love; the burial chamber in Egypt filled with wrapped bodies, and the painted face on the sarcophagus lid, like a sick woman raising her head from the pillow; 'a night and a day I have been in the abyss'. What abyss? What step had I jumped? Where had been the milestone and the iron dome? There? Not there. Where?

As I sat in the dining-room, while the waitresses trooped in through the swing doors carrying their laden trays, I sometimes began to feel panic; my heart thumped, as if in a few moments I should be compelled to stand up at my solitary table and shout I didn't know what.

In the evening the fear was absent when I talked and drank café kirsch with Frau Professor Heinz and the friendly American, and thought that my father would be wondering because the cheques I drew were so much larger than the standard sanatorium charges. Sometimes Frau Heinz and I played piano arrangements of Haydn symphonies. I played badly and nothing marked faster than *andante* could be taken at anything like the proper speed; but as I had a good sense of time and left out what I couldn't play, and as Frau Heinz considerately listened to hear how I was getting on, the music maintained its movement and I was often carried away by it. When the symphony was finished, and with our hands in our laps we turned and smiled at each other, I felt well and happy. 'You only become yourself through music,' she once said. David again, I thought. *Cave musicam*, Nietzsche had warned.

Part of the day I still tried to find the meaning of the milestone and the steps, which appeared in all the trains of association to all my dreams. I filled pages and pages of notebooks with the images that came too quickly for me to seize them

92

all. I couldn't tell when to stop, for I couldn't tell when I had reached the dream's meaning. I didn't know whether it was a symbol of what I wanted to be or to do or to have, of what I wanted or of what I didn't want. In dreams as in music, somebody had said, there is no way of saying 'no'. Even to say 'No' in words, I thought, is still an act; it is impossible to be a negation. That idea, I thought, like my power of resistance, comes from Konrad.

One evening in January, 1926, when I came out of the dining-room – one descended to it from the ground floor, for the sanatorium was built on a slope and the dining-room faced down the hill – I felt the whole internal mass of the building impending upon me; and in sudden alarm and frantic desire for relief I went to the patients' lending library, which till now I had scorned. I took out John Buchan's *The Three Hostages,* went to my room, got into bed, and began to read. I read on and on, till it was past midnight, and I was still reading. I read until I finished the book in the small hours, the ashtray beside my bed full of cigarette butts.

No book I call good, I thought, ever held me like that. What had held me now? Not only the excitement of the story, but the living vicariously through Dick Hannay, an Englishman and a gentleman. That is the truth about me. One look at me and everybody knows I am English; and I believe myself a gentleman.

The room, like my mouth, was stale with smoke. I threw open the windows and the night air flowed in like water, cold from the snow. If I bared my breast to it I could make my lungs bad again. The thought didn't interest me. Moving the window back and forth, I ventilated the room so that the doctor on his morning round should not smell the smoke. Then turning out the light, I settled down, not to dream, but to sleep.

In February I was allowed to go down to Zürich to get teeth made. I was told to take the greatest care; there was influenza about, and an infection would set me back months.

I came out of the station with my bag and as I walked down the new crowded street, I thought of the inmates of the sanatorium far away up in the mountains and was glad that nobody knew me to be one of them, though I also felt as if I were an unappreciated traveller from a strange land.

After I had had my mouth crammed full with the clayey sickening mess, there were some days to wait before the teeth were ready, and I stayed in a small old hotel in an arcaded street looking over the river Limmat. On the ground floor there was a busy and unpretentious restaurant where I had my meals and made notes of the shrewd, solid, jovial faces, like those carved on medieval altar screens, and read the papers, and thought I should know more about Trotsky and Stalin and about the strike of the miners, of whose short-sighted obstinacy my father had written to me.

Though I felt as if I might be getting flu, I went to hear Mozart's *Entführung aus dem Serail*. I was so taken out of myself that next day, though I had a fairly high temperature, I sat up in bed to write about it. I felt restored and well; in the opera there was no negation; all, good and bad, had been transmuted into the beauty of music and sang together.

In a couple of days I was up again, and the chamber-maid who had looked after me, a big, good-tempered country girl, told me how handsome I should be with my new teeth. When I got them and tried to eat, my mouth seemed full of rocks.

As the train went up the mountains again, I felt uneasiness as if I were returning home. But when I was summoned by the doctors next day for examination, I didn't tell them that I had been in bed with flu, but on a sudden impulse asked to see the chart of my lungs, which they had taken out of my file. 'Do you think you can understand it?' I was asked. 'I think so,' I replied. The affected parts were marked in red, which had been covered over with black cross-hatching as the lung healed, and now only a small patch of red remained.

I continued to play duets with Frau Heinz, and at hours when nobody was likely to be about I practised easy pieces of Bach and Haydn from a beginners' album I had bought in Zürich. One evening in March I was going back to my room up the wide echoing stairs and saw the head doctor and his assistant on the corridor of the floor above. I was whistling a phrase from a piece I had been practising, when the head doctor called out, like a German policeman, 'Silence there!' I have had enough of this, I thought.

A couple of weeks later I moved to a hotel at the other end of the village, where was the sound of loud, laughing voices as men and girls returned from ski-ing. I began again a novel about myself in the German village before the war.

In the lowlands it would now be spring, so I walked down the long loops of the road into the valley. The snow disappeared and on the green slopes there were copses of beech with a purplish bloom. Then I took the train back into the mountains and the surviving winter; and even here, on the sunny slopes, the purple and white crocuses were piercing through the patchy snow.

But I wished that I could arrest time. Like the ass's skin in Balzac's story, the red patch on my lungs was shrinking and soon I would have to come out of this retreat from the world. I added up the sums on the stubs in my cheque book, and found that I had cost my father nearly £300, at which I felt my heart beating. The doctors to whom I still went for examination told me I should stay at least another three months, but I didn't believe them.

'You must start thinking about the future,' my father wrote. I ought to go back to Berlin and to Paul, I thought. But I didn't want to. Then in early May Frau Heinz told me that a Swiss business man had asked her husband, who was a lawyer in Zürich, if he could recommend an Englishman who would be willing to live in his house and teach him English. So I said I would be glad to go.

The business-man – his name was Zwingli – lived in a good-sized villa on a hillside outside Zürich, overlooking the lake. I had arrived in the afternoon and been kindly greeted by Frau Zwingli, and had made friends with her children, Felix, who told me that in a week he would be five, and his sister, Heidi, just turned three; and I had been growled at and sulkily accepted by an obese French bull-terrier. When we were having tea in the garden, Herr Zwingli returned from his office. He came across the lawn with his hand outstretched. 'Welcome to my house,' he said.

We were supposed to do English every evening after supper. Having taken off his collar and tie, and settled himself with coffee and kirsch beside him and his feet up on a chair, he translated, drawing on his cheroot, the sentences I read out from the old-fashioned grammar he insisted on our using; and with a brooding, uninterested look in his blue eyes he listened

95

to my explanations of his numerous mistakes. After half-an-hour or less he would say in Swiss German, 'A daft bloody language', and tell his wife to bring some wine and me to put a record on the gramophone. Then, after I had been there a fortnight or so, his wife would look at me, cocking an eyebrow and twirling a forefinger, and among the solid furniture we would dance to 'Valencia'.

I sat beside Herr Zwingli in his car as he drove about northern and central Switzerland, calling at factories, banks and big hotels to demonstrate the calculating machine of which he was the agent. I did what I could to make English conversation, but soon we were speaking German. Though he sometimes recited to me, as if I were a prospective buyer, the beauties of mechanization and rationalization, to which I responded with shameless adaptations of Spengler's theories of Caesarean finance, I felt that he only half believed in what he said. He came of old Swiss peasant stock and had been born and brought up in the mountains; and there, I thought, he belonged, and not in the world of the unpredictable market which his wife and children, safe and unknowing in their home, trusted him to master. 'You can think yourself lucky, Mr West,' he sometimes said. 'You have no ties.'

But though it eased him to talk to me, he condemned such freedom as mine. He let me feel that no man of my age and education should be a retainer in another man's house; and he told me that if I set about it with energy, an Englishman with my qualifications could make a fine career for himself in Switzerland and marry and settle down. And on a Saturday evening, after he had teased the dog, which he, with his obstinate mouth, resembled, and played with Felix and Heidi till they shrieked with delight, and sworn at his wife, Meta, to show that his mood was good, his eyes were shining with proud content as he told me to fetch the grammar for 'a bit of English'.

Not long after I came to Zürich, Cecil wrote to me that a daughter had been born to them. I wrote to tell him how glad I was. As I wrote and reflected, I remembered how Graeme and Cecil and I had once been walking along Archway Road, after riding on the first run of the new Barnet tram, when a street urchin came towards us, and Cecil, in one of his larking moods, had dodged from side to side on the pavement so that the boy couldn't pass; and I had thought that of the three of us Cecil alone could have done that. Without my knowing why, it seemed right to tell him of the memory, and I did so. And I congratulated my father that he was a grandfather now in reality, instead of in my bedtime fantasy of George, Arthur and Birt.

In my abundant free time I went on with the novel I had begun in the mountains, and I read what I had written to Frau Heinz. She had returned to Zürich to be psycho-analyzed by a follower of Jung, since she thought that her continuing evening temperature might be caused by unconscious conflict. We talked about the General Strike in England, and I told her of my suspicion, which had come into my mind from somewhere or other, that the Government had provoked it. 'What a diabolical notion!' she exclaimed. She will have no criticism of governments, I thought; to talk about the unconscious motives of individuals makes conversations interesting, but governments are what they say they are. While I suspected that she saw herself being Frau von Stein to the only available substitute for Goethe, I listened to her sensible criticism that in my novel I should 'vary the nothings', by which she meant the continual opening and shutting of doors, and similar actions.

For an hour or so after my late breakfast, while Frau Zwingli and her old mother did the housework, I played the piano. Heidi used to come and thump on the bass, and Frau Zwingli sometimes came and listened. She encouraged me to play because, she said, it helped me in my 'dark moods'. I spent a good many hours at an exhibition of Rembrandt's etchings, and thought that in them also was a power like that of music to transcend negation and to give to everything and to everyone, dead or living, beggar or rich, man and woman, young, aged and deformed, the reality of being. I went with Frau Zwingli to see a Russian film, *Cruiser Potemkin*, which left a permanent memory of the crawling carcases that were the sailors' food, the relentless tread of the Czar's soldiers and the perambulator bumping down the steps before them, and the sailors' unyielding will and courage. Outside the cinema there were two men selling a paper, *Die Rote Fahne*, and that sight also remained.

One night, as I was lying in bed, I was wondering if I was schizophrenic, and then remembered that only a few moments before I had been thinking that perhaps I had picked up a flea from the dog, Alex. I was curious how my mind had moved from the flea to the schizophrenia, and recalled a book I had looked at when I was in Berlin – *Das vorbewusste phantasierende Denken,* by Varendonck. If I now made notes of such trains of association, I might be able to find out what made the movement of thought and so find out the truth about myself. Soon I could retrace a train of thought which, though it had only lasted a minute or so, would fill several pages of the small notebook I kept beside my bed. But I knew that to get at the energy that moved the mind from one image to the next I would have to go deeper than pre-conscious fantasy. Then the fear of the milestone returned and of the step that I had jumped; and one day in Zürich I thought that a man getting on to a tram was myself; and though I knew quite well he wasn't, it gave a peculiar jerk to my mind. And as I was repeatedly bringing myself back to full consciousness to recover trains of thought, I began to suffer from insomnia. So after some weeks I gave up.

The summer was passing. August 1st was the great Swiss national holiday, and by the time the day came I had sat so many hours beside Herr Zwingli as he drove through the Swiss cantons that I understood something of what the day meant for him; and for a week or more Felix had been telling me that in so and so many days it would be the first of August.

While the children stayed at home in the charge of their grandmother, Herr Zwingli drove with his wife to Schaffhausen and asked me to come with them. There was to be open-air dancing on the top of the Munot Turm, an old tower about a hundred feet high, with room for seventy or eighty couples on its flat roof, ringed with crenellated battlements. It was a beautiful summer night, and in the hazy sky there was a large golden moon. There was no other light except the shaded lamps of the small orchestra of violins, double-bass and accordion seated in the centre. Round and round, always in the same direction. with a rhythmic shuffling of their feet upon the stone, moved the dancers, while other pairs leaned against the battlements and watched them, or, turning their backs, looked out across the small town. A speech was made in honour of the day, and all drank together to their country. We stayed till about three in the morning, and then drove home. Dawn had broken as we came over the hills to the north of Zürich and saw the lake beneath us. Herr Zwingli stopped the car and we got out. It seemed as if mankind had not yet come to the earth, except that there was a small white sail far out on the lake.

CHAPTER VIII

In September, 1926, I heard that the post of Lektor for English at Basle University was vacant. I applied and was appointed. My duties were to give classes in conversation, phonetics and grammar, amounting to six hours weekly, and one lecture a week on English life and literature. I continued to live in Herr Zwingli's house, spending one night a week in Basle, as I had agreed to teach him until the end of the year. I then moved to Basle and took rooms with a clergyman's widow in what was known as the aristocratic quarter of the town.

Before the spring term began, I went to Berlin for a week to see Paul.

He told me that when he had got my letter saying that I had taken the post in Basle, he had thought to himself that it was characteristic of me. I had settled myself in Basle when I could have made as good a living in Berlin and in a much more challenging atmosphere; for with the rise of the German National Socialist Labour Party, Berlin was the centre of the deepening crisis of Western culture. 'But you want to be left alone,' he said, 'and you don't like fighting. That's why you have never really freed yourself from your family. Now, as English lecturer in a small Swiss town, you'll have the security and the social position which will please them and yourself, and you'll do your work conscientiously.' Then he talked of the work we could do together on 'the three realities'.

On my way to the University, carrying what my students, as I later learned, called my 'Hebammetäschli', or midwife's bag, I crossed the Cathedral Square, its wide space cobbled with brownish stones between which here and there grew blades of grass. On three sides were eighteenth century houses with curving wrought iron before their lower windows. In the north-east corner was the warm red sandstone of the Cathedral. On the west front, standing out from the wall upon a plinth, was the statue of a young woman with a big round apple in her raised hand, her figure lithe and free beneath the folds of the drapery, and a pleased smile on her tilted, rather chubby face; but on either side of the north door the gaunt forms of patriarchs and prophets were still constricted within the stone fabric. For they had been carved when the group was still supreme, but the statue of the girl expressed the freedom of the individual. That was what Paul would say. So long as I stood still and looked, I felt that in Paul's idea of the changing spirit of Western culture was the truth of what I saw. Yet when I moved and walked on and people passed me, it became irrelevant.

I felt that in the town was a different life. In the beginning of Lent, Carneval was held. The opening ceremony was on the Marktplatz at five in the morning, and Herr Zwingli had told me on no account to miss it. So I got up in good time and started walking. There was no traffic in the dark streets, only people in twos and threes all going in the same direction, as if to a mysterious assembly. But opposing them, holding them up for a moment, pawing at their breasts, then leaping away to cut off another group, were fantastic figures with heads of bears, cocks, dogs. A human cat pinned on my overcoat the Carneval badge, and I forked out money. On the Marktplatz, under the tall arc lights, the cobbled space where the stalls were set up on market days was packed with people. There was little movement and no sound except a low murmur and from the small streets that converged upon the square the muffled roll of drums.

As the clock of the Town Hall struck five, all the street lights went out. The roof of artificial darkness above them was rent and the sky broke open, and in a moment a few stars appeared. The roll of drums grew louder, and presently from the side-streets huge rectangular lanterns slowly advanced upon us. Carried on long poles by animal figures, preceded and followed by masked drummers, they displayed on their painted and illuminated sides savage caricatures of the Basle Government (for the town was an independent Canton), the leaders of the political parties, rich and notorious citizens and their wives and mistresses. The people shouted and clapped and hooted, and the drumming went on and on till the last lantern had disappeared and the lights came on again, and the people flooded the streets as they thronged to the cafés to drink hot brown soup, and the trams clanged their bells.

After that morning, I continually thought that behind the daily appearance of the streets was the life which could thus manifest itself with an imagination as fantastic as that of the Egyptian tombs. And I thought that though Paul had said I was hiding myself behind my social position in a town where nothing happened, there was in this town a peculiar tension between the cathedral of God standing high on rising ground and the drumming on the Marktplatz below as the illuminated lanterns following each other out of the darkness ridiculed all authority.

I felt tension also as in the course of the summer white-washed slogans appeared on walls in the drab streets of the industrial quarter 'Befreit Sacco and Vanzetti'. One evening I had been asked to the house of Dr Oettinger, public prosecutor in the Basle courts, to whom Frau Heinz had given me an introduction. He was friendly, though reserved, his face striking in its resemblance to Baudelaire; we used to meet for lunch in a tea-shop, where he had a glass of hot milk and a couple of sandwiches he brought from home. On this evening we were talking after supper about the poet Stefan George, whom he admired and I disliked, when his telephone rang. 'Hier Oettinger,' he said, leaning back in his chair. He listened, and then he crouched low over the instrument. He got up from his chair, the receiver still to his ear. 'On the Barfüssliplatz? Yes. Yes. I'm coming right away.' As he replaced the receiver, he said hurriedly to his wife, 'Some lunatics have tried to blow up the tram-stop. Sacco and Vanzetti, of course. I don't know when I shall be back. You stay, Herr West.' He left, changed before my eyes into the public prosecutor.

I went regularly to the tea-room for lunch and generally Dr Oettinger was there, sometimes with colleagues from the law-courts, whose conversation, since it was in Swiss German and often about local affairs, I followed with difficulty. But they were friendly, and if they saw me interested in their talk they changed to High German. Once I got into excited discussion with the assistant prosecutor on a film we had both seen about a husband obsessed with the desire to sever the nape of his wife's neck. The advertisements claimed, and the Assistant prosecutor agreed, that the film brought Freud on to the screen; but in fact it exploited him. When I apologized for having become heated, the assistant prosecutor said, 'To get at the truth make the witness angry'.

102

It was not only anger that had quickened my speech. In the group round the table was a girl of about my own age. She had taken no part in the discussion but had watched me. Dr Oettinger and she seemed to know each other well, and in his manner to her there was a respectful consideration and a careful and rallying kindness. When I was accompanying him part of the way back to the Law Courts, I asked him who she was. He said that her name was Sophie Huber, that she was a teacher, and that she had many difficulties.

A few days later, when I went to the tea-room for lunch, she was sitting alone in a corner, and I asked if I might join her. She smiled hard, drawing her upper lip back across her teeth, and said, 'Yes'.

She told me that she taught a class of deaf children. It must be solitary, I said, to talk and to know that her voice was not being heard. 'They read from my lips,' she answered.

She told me that her father had been head of a school for training missionaries for Africa, and I said that my father had been a missionary in India; two years ago her father – a widower – had died, but already before his death she had gone into a flat of her own because, she said, she wanted to be free. That, I thought, will be what Dr Oettinger meant when he spoke of her difficulties.

We talked of music. At the State Theatre Mozart's opera *Bastien and Bastienne* was being done by the Viennese Sängerknaben. 'Would you like to come and see it with me?' I asked her. In the same instant as I spoke, remembering that in dreams to go to the theatre may be, according to Freud's interpretation, a symbol of marrying, my body desired, as it desired that first time in my father's study when I read in the Bible how Absalom had lain with his sister. Erect, I waited for her answer. She said that she would like to come, and we arranged time and place.

As I walked up and down at the street corner where we were to meet, I thought that my stepmother would approve her because she was a lady and because, even though she had left home, she had, I thought, a sense of family; and between her and my stepmother I thought I could see some likeness of determined vitality, as in a plant growing in thin soil. I said to myself in German: 'Objektwahl durch die Stiefmutter bedingt'

103

– choice of object determined by the stepmother. I know it, but I go on waiting.

She came half running, because she was a little late, turning her feet out as girls were told to do when I was a boy. She was wearing a hat of fine black straw which made her look as if she were in the Salvation Army; and when we shook hands, I saw that there was fresh powder in the wings of her nostrils, which touched me. In the best restaurant we had supper of cold salmon with a Swiss white wine, and then wild strawberries. From the way she held her head I could feel the tension in her neck and shoulders, though at moments delight and triumph flashed in her grey-blue eyes and she kept glancing round the restaurant, till I wondered whether she was anxious to see if anyone was there who knew her.

We arrived at the theatre in good time, and made our way to our seats. When we had read all we wanted of the programme, she looked at the people coming in from every side and settling themselves and talking and smiling with their heads turned in profile to each other, and said, 'Everybody is specially dressed for the evening at the theatre and they are all friendly. Don't you like it too?'

After a week or so, she rang up and said a friend of hers, Emilie, was coming to coffee on the following evening and would I like to join them. Her flat was on the top floor of a block on the same estate as Dr Oettinger's house. When in response to my ring she had pressed the button that made the street door buzz and open and I was mounting the narrow concrete stairs, I heard her feet racing down. Her face was eager and anxious, and her eyes alight, as she slowed and stopped, two or three steps above me, and said, 'Emilie couldn't come. Do you mind?' I wondered, as I followed her up the stairs, whether she had invited her.

She gave me excellent coffee and a glass of kirsch, and talked of Emilie, daughter of a famous classical scholar. 'Emilie will introduce you to her father,' she said, 'and you will meet other professors and that will be useful. Only this evening you must make do with me.'

Her legs curled beneath her, she was sitting at one end of a divan, and I at the other, with my coffee and kirsch on a black Finnish table. She was wearing a plain frock of very fine wool, smocked at the waist, an indefinable shade of deep pink, which yet seemed to bring out both the blue in her grey-blue eyes and a gold sheen in her dark brown hair. Remembering the hat she had worn when we went to the theatre, I wondered that she had chosen such a lovely colour. And the pure colours of the cushions of Shantung silk on the black divan, the rich Kelim carpet on the dark green floor, so filled the small low room that it did not seem to need the light coming through the window from the paling summer sky.

'Do you like my flat? Come,' she said, 'I'll show you the other room.' The colours were richer and darker, and the room was more withdrawn. She pointed to a couch covered with a Persian rug. 'That is where I sleep,' she said, 'only I don't'. On one wall was a reproduction of Dürer's *Melancholia*. 'I have his *Knight, Death and the Devil*,' I said, and felt that it was bad to say it, because I was beginning a flattering mythology.

'And this is my spinet,' she said, moving her hand to and fro on the old polished wood, and I noticed again the frayed skin on the side of her forefinger. 'And these are my duets,' she went on, 'Mozart and Haydn symphonies, Handel's Organ Concertos. I bound them myself.' I took the volumes in my hands and admired the precision of the gold lines along the join of the cloth and the leather corner-pieces. 'Shall we play something? You like to take the bass, you said, didn't you?' We chose a Haydn symphony. She played much better than I, but still as if her music mistress were standing behind her.

We went back into the other room. 'I'll just make some more coffee,' she said, and left me. Free to think, I looked at her room, and wondered who she was.

'It's not late,' she said. 'Only half-past nine. I needn't be quiet till ten.' And she wound up the gramophone and put on a fox-trot. 'Let's dance,' I said. Our cheeks touched, and remained touching; and while the finished record continued with a tone-less scraping to revolve, we stood, cheek pressing against cheek, my arm round her. I kissed her. 'I don't like your name – Sophie,' I said. 'What can I call you?' 'Sonja,' she answered.

She stopped the gramophone and turned off the light, and we lay down on the divan. Again I wondered; for her kissing was experienced. 'Let's undress,' I said; but she wouldn't. We lay in each other's arms, hardly speaking. I wondered whether to say 'I love you', but said nothing.

About eleven o'clock she said, 'I'll see you some of the way home', and we went out into a warm summer night. Where the houses ended we passed a field of ripening corn, and I picked a long stalk and carried it upright in my hand, and gently stroked her cheek with the ear. 'Alick, Alick,' she said in a low voice, and then no more. I had felt happy and had talked of the loveliness of the night, but the happiness was ebbing and I couldn't find any more words. We walked slowly on, her weight growing heavier on my arm; and remembering Oettinger's words, I was uneasy.

The next day we were to have supper together and to meet outside the Cathedral. Sonja had asked me not to be late because she hated waiting, so I arrived well before the time. I looked at the statue of the girl on the west front and the tall forms of the saints and prophets, and then I walked beneath the chestnut trees near the Cathedral, and looked across the Rhine and the roofs to the hills of the Black Forest and Germany invisible beyond them.

I saw Sonja coming and hastened to meet her. We went down a steep path to the ferry over the Rhine, for we were going to have supper in a restaurant on the other bank. The ferry was a flat, blunt barge; the force of the river carried it across, for it was attached by a steel rope to a cable that ran from bank to bank about twenty feet above the water, and when the steersman brought it broadside on to the weight of the current, it surged forward against the rushing, swirling water, and the Cathedral and the houses on either bank wheeled around us as we sat in the bow.

We had a table on the restaurant terrace beside a balustrade with red geraniums and blue lobelias, and we looked across the Rhine to the silhouette of the old town. When we spoke, I felt the word 'Du' like a caress. I told her about Ruhleben and the Arts and Science Union and my acting, and that I had written poetry. Beneath an absence of ordinary conversational comment she was listening intently, and I was curious how she was thinking of me.

There were silences; and once she said unexpectedly, scraping at something on her plate, that her sister was going to be married at the end of July – which was in a fortnight or so. I talked of the woman with the apple and of the patriarchs on the Cathedral, and of Paul's idea that we should write a history of the three phases of Western culture. She listened with lowered eyes. 'You believe that will help people?' she asked. Which was to me such a strange idea that I had no answer.

She asked me if I would be going to Berlin to see Paul in the summer vacation. I said that I was going to England, as I hadn't been home for nearly two years, but that I would not be going for another month or so yet. Then I found myself saying what had been in my mind: 'Let you and me go away somewhere together'. 'Alick, I don't know,' she answered.

We met again a few days later, and again Sonja spoke of her sister's approaching marriage. The man was a clergyman, and the wedding would be in a little town not far from Lake Constance. I asked her if she was going, and she said, 'No'. Rather shocked, I asked her if her sister would not be hurt, and suggested that she should go to the wedding and we then have some days on Lake Constance. No, she answered, it wouldn't do. Schmid had said she shouldn't go. 'Who is Schmid?' I asked. She replied that he was a doctor, a friend of Jung, who helped her when things were difficult. Half resenting this rival, half uneasy, I said, 'Go all the same, and then meet me'. Late one evening she rang up and said that she would come.

I arrived in the village the day before, and in a quiet, secluded house, which was the annexe of the hotel, took for a week two pleasant rooms.

Thinking I would do some work before she came, I had brought the notes of the lectures I had given in the summer term on Defoe and Fielding, which I meant to write up in the vacation.

But I couldn't work. Whether I thought of my lectures or of the morrow, I was apprehensive. In my lectures, I had used Paul's theory of 'the three realities': the novel was the literary form which arose when the group lost its organic unity; Robinson Crusoe, the individual, himself mastered the world. But what most moved me was Crusoe's fear of having done wrong in disobeying his father, and his dream, when he was ill, of a man with a spear raised to pierce him; and he would be pierced in his right side, as Christ was pierced, or as Jacob's thigh was touched by the angel with whom he wrestled in Gauguin's picture.

I couldn't work. I could only wait for Sonja.

She arrived late in the afternoon of the next day, and we went and sat in a field beside the lake. She was excited, and described the church and the ceremony and the reception, and said that her sister had been pleased that she had come, and that I had been right to tell her that she should not stay away.

She laid her hand in mine as we sat on the grass. 'It is good to talk to you,' she said; 'you are so calm.' I noticed that she had cut her forefinger, and thought that she had done it to enact on herself, both as the woman and as the man, the deflowering of her sister on the wedding night. For her, all our week together would be in rivalry with her sister, who was two years younger than she. I thought that when I had suggested we should meet, I had known well that, coming straight to me from her sister's wedding, she must inevitably identify and contrast our being thus together with our being husband and wife; and yet I had made the proposal.

I sat beside her, holding her hand in mine and feeling that she was drawing comfort from me. 'I shouldn't have begun,' I thought, 'but now how can I stop?'

Sonja changed her dress and we went to the hotel for dinner, and in a large room filled with holidaying families we sat at a small table by ourselves. After a stroll, we went back to the annexe, which except for us was empty. I wanted her, and we undressed and kissed, but she would not let me make love.

All next day we spent on the lake, picnicking on the bank, bathing and taking photographs of each other, now and then kissing, and we were lulled by the gentle rowing through the calm bright water and under overhanging trees. 'Do you know what day it is tomorrow?' Sonja asked. 'It's the First of August. Do you know what that means to us?' I told her about the dancing on the Munot Turm and the drive back in the early morning, but no more. She had asked me if I had loved other women, and I had said that I had.

That night she kissed me more passionately, and then stopped, and said, with a nervous laugh, almost as if she still believed it, 'Till I was nearly twenty, I thought women got babies from kissing'.

She came to my bed next morning, like a child on her birthday, and wished us 'A happy First of August', and said we must help everybody to be happy. Again we spent the day on the lake, but we were less at peace, and part of the afternoon Sonja dozed, because she had slept badly the night before. But when she got ready to go to the hotel for dinner and the celebration of the holiday, she was animated and I tried to feel like her.

The dining-room was gay with decorations and on each table was the Swiss flag. Voices were livelier, and there was talking and laughing from table to table. Sonja and I and a middle-aged couple near us raised our glasses to each other. Towards the end of the meal the proprietor of the hotel made a speech, and we all rose and drank to 'our dear Switzerland'. As we sat down, I said to Sonja, 'I should tell them that there was an Englishman drinking with them'. 'Oh, yes, Alick, yes, Alick,' she cried excitedly, and struck on her glass with her knife, and not listening to me said to the waitress, 'Herr West, an Englishman, would like to speak. Please tell the proprietor.' The proprietor rose. 'We have with us an English guest who would like to say a few words. Herr West.' I stood up in a dead silence. I said that I hoped they would not feel that I, as an Englishman, had had no right to drink with them, but I would like to thank them for the hospitality and friendliness I had enjoyed in Switzerland and to tell them that an Englishman also wished their country happiness. There was applause and I sat down; and as I felt the curious looks from other tables, I asked Sonja, 'Was that all right?' She said with shining eyes, 'Very good, Alick; very, very good'.

When dinner was over and the daylight was already fading, many of the guests, we following them, went down to the small harbour, where there were rowing boats with red Chinese lanterns. I rowed Sonja slowly out from the shore, the blades of the oars gently pressing against the firm water, and in the seat at the stern she leaned forwards, dangling the lantern on the end of its stick. It became darker on the water, and the lanterns glowed from the other boats, and there came the sound of singing. 'I thank you, Alick,' Sonja said.

I asked her if she would like to go to dance, but she said, no, she was happy, but she didn't feel very well. So I rowed her

109

back, and we went to our rooms. 'Kiss me goodnight,' she said. 'I've taken one of my pills, and I shall have a good night. But leave your door open.'

I went to my room. I smoked a cigarette, and thought of what I had done. 'We have with us an English guest who would like to . . . ' I shook my head in disbelief.

There was no sound from Sonja's room, which opened out of mine, and I soon fell asleep. I wakened before daybreak and thought I heard something, and lay listening. Sonja was crying. I turned on the light and went to her. She clung to me, and said, the words pouring out, broken by sobbing, 'Alick, help me, help me. He said I shouldn't have come. I told you. I'm going mad. I'm going mad.'

I managed to quieten her a little and, not knowing what else to do, made her take another of her sleeping pills.

She woke late, and I took her over to the hotel for breakfast. The few guests still in the dining-room looked round with friendly interest, but Sonja seemed hardly aware of them. When we got back to our room, I thought I had better take her out; for in privacy with me nothing would oblige her to control herself. I didn't like to row her on the lake, for fear of what she might do; so we walked slowly along a lane to the next village.

She talked in a flat voice, her eyes half closed; or, sinking into silence, she hung her dead weight on me. When we got to the village, she said, 'Now we'll go into the church'. We sat in a pew, not touching each other, and Sonja looked all the time towards the altar, which was decorated with flowers. Through the open door could be heard the sound of men doing road repairs in the sunlight outside, and as we came out and passed them, the shafts of a cart were tilted up and its load of grey stones tipped out. Sonja said, in the same flat voice, 'That is a noise in hell'. At her words I heard the sound through her, and I wondered with a sense of awe at the intensity of perception with which she was now living beside me.

Next day she had let herself go still more, and continually wanted reassurance that she need not fear she would have a child. Yet at meals in the hotel dining-room she could talk and attract no attention, and I thought what power was being exerted by her upbringing. But fearing that her state would get worse, and knowing that she had a brother in Basle who was house physician at the hospital, I said that we would go back the following day, and she made no resistance.

I took first class tickets so that we should be alone in the carriage. She leaned against me with her eyes closed, and once in a drowsy voice she said, 'I am your bride'.

CHAPTER IX

When after two or three weeks Sonja was allowed to return from the mental hospital where her brother had sent her, I went frequently to see her. We played duets, and went out for walks. She made an album for the photographs we had taken on Lake Constance and painted on the cover a bright pattern with straight five-petalled flowers.

Dr Oettinger asked me what had happened, and from what he told me I understood why I had felt a closeness between him and Sonja. Three years before she had tried to commit suicide by taking an overdose of sleeping powder, but she had written to him of her intention and he had come in time to bring her back to life; since then he and his wife had regularly asked her to their house and kept watch on her. His manner to me was considerate, but I felt in it a reprimand for irresponsibility in setting up myself against Dr Schmid, who, he told me, wished to see me.

Dr Schmid had a house outside Basle, near the German frontier. He was a man of stature, with a shock of iron-grey hair, and watchful, guarded dark-brown eyes, with a divergent squint. His first words were that I had come through a difficult and testing experience; was I able to talk about it? Not much liking the question, I told him what had happened, including my interpretation of why Sonja had cut her finger. Then he said, 'You still love her?' Unwillingly, but without hesitation, I answered that I did.

He then said that I must not blame myself for having persuaded Sonja to go to her sister's wedding. He had advised her not to go because to see her younger sister being married might release a surge of energy from the depths of her being too strong for the defences she had built against it. If that energy had no aim nor hope, it would have turned inwards and might have done her great harm. But now it was turned towards me. 'Even if you would consider it,' he concluded, 'this is not the time to think of marriage; but if you can, let her live through you.'

Waiting in the sunlight for the tram to take me back to

Basle, I looked across a great field of bare stubble and quivering air, beyond which was a line of tall trees. Nothing was passing on the road, and I thought in the stillness that I must and could let Sonja live through me.

At home, where I arrived early in September, I felt relieved from a strain, though every day on the silver tray in the hall there was a heavy envelope, addressed in the small, tight, pressed handwriting which made a sheet of her letters, despite the space between the lines, appear impenetrably thick with urgent words. My stepmother, I thought, would be sure to have noticed, but nothing was said. I was let go my own way; and since I appeared now to be at the start of a career, it was to be hoped that things would turn out well for me after all.

We had moved from West Hill to a beautiful Georgian house in Southwood Lane with a long, sloping garden from which one could see for miles over north-east London. My father, now nearing seventy, worked in it for five or six hours a day, and I sometimes helped him in the afternoons, after working at my lectures in the morning. There was pleasure and friendliness between us as we had tea on the flagged terrace outside the french windows of the dining-room. Once he got up from his chair to hold out to me the plate of cucumber sandwiches 'Arthur!' exclaimed my stepmother, 'don't wait on your son.' He said in a fierce voice, 'We like to do things for each other.'

I saw Paul, his parents having moved to North Finchley. He asked me what I was going to lecture on in the winter term, and I said that I thought I ought to tell my students something about England. The suspicion started in my mind by the General Strike had not been completely silenced, and I had been reading Webb's *History of Trade Unionism*. It seemed to me, I said to Paul, that the occurrence of sporadic strikes and short-lived associations already in the thirteenth and fourteenth centuries raised problems about the reality of the organic group. 'Do they make the cathedral any the less real?' he asked. Then he said, 'You are hiding something.'

Sonja was there to meet me at the station, and we went to her flat. The table was laid for supper, and on my napkin she had put petals of the last roses from her small patch in the gardens shared by the flat-dwellers. She was more calm, and her voice was warm and less constricted. But we only kissed for a little while, for I felt that she was like a child that is consciously being good.

She was living her ordinary life again, and teaching her deaf children. Once a week she was going to Dr Schmid, but I didn't ask her about their talks, nor did she tell me anything except that he said she should think herself fortunate that it was I with whom she had gone away – which I heard with a mingling of vanity and a scepticism directed both at myself and him. He had also advised her to do more book-binding and to take up another craft she had practised, which was that of lettering. So she asked me to bring her some of my poems so that she could write them out in a fine script on a beautiful handmade paper and bind them in finely grained leather, whose colour I must choose.

We went into the other room, where I noticed she had taken down Dürer's *Melancholia,* and played duets. Before I left I unpacked from my bag a small Persian rug I had brought for her and put it down beside her bed. But I saw that for some reason I could not understand she had become unhappy and hurt, and I wondered with misgiving what I had done wrong.

A fortnight or so later she told me. She asked me to tea to meet her friend, Emilie. I wondered what could be the bond between Sonja and her, for Emilie was large, square, stupid and managing, and told me that I should have called on all the professors in the faculty of Arts to pay my respects. When she had gone, Sonja gave me an envelope, and said, 'There's a present for you'. Inside there was a subscription ticket for a series of concerts to be given during the winter by the Basle Municipal Orchestra, conducted by Weingartner. I was delighted. But in the same moment I saw that in the envelope there was a second ticket, and the expression of my face must have changed, for I thought immediately that Sonja cared nothing about the music, but wanted us to be seen together at the great occasion of the town's social life. I thanked her, but she said in a crushed voice, 'You would rather go alone'. 'No, I wouldn't,' I said, and tried to comfort her, knowing that what she said was true. She sat beside me in dejection. After some time she said, 'You brought me the carpet for my room, but

114

you don't give yourself. I must stay here, and wait.' That is unjust, I thought, but I was ashamed.

We went to the concerts, at first as if we were sitting beside each other after a quarrel, but with each week the strain relaxed. Every two or three weeks Sonja came to my room for tea, which the clergyman's widow brought in. She liked Sonja and had known her father slightly, and after she had set out the tea she would stand and talk with the empty tray in her hand. Sonja always brought flowers, and she made cushions to brighten the room with colour. She had chosen ten of my poems, saying nothing about them, and written them out in a beautiful Italian script and bound them in blue saffian leather.

By the time the concerts were over, Carneval was approaching. Sonja said she could not stay in Basle when the town went mad, so she was going away into the mountains with Emilie. Before she left I went to her flat one afternoon. We made love for the first time, and I was surprised and uneasy because afterwards Sonja talked as if nothing unusual had happened.

In the weeks that followed she outwardly kept her docile manner, but I felt forming itself within her a personal independence. Through resources in herself, not through any comfort drawn from me, she had overcome the shock of losing her virginity and yet not being able to give herself to me because of her obsessive fear of a child and because I was not a husband.

That fear she never overcame; but she accepted, and answered for it to herself, that we were lovers without being married. She had become more mature, and she said nothing to me of the effort that had cost her. Behind her quiet submissive manner and the generous smiling welcome when I came to her flat for supper at a table decked as if she only lived for my coming, I thought there was the working of a character stronger than my own. Sometimes I wondered whether her unresisting compliance was to be a quicksand for me. At other times I felt in her a resentment and rancour because I had destroyed the independent person who had won freedom from her home, and I heard in her voice a critically observant tone when she said to me one day, when we had been talking of Schmid, 'I thought you were calm, but you're not. I think you have your difficulties, too.'

115

In the early summer I went to Dr Schmid myself – why, I could not have said.

He began by asking me what was the last dream I remembered. It was of a queen seated on a throne, and on each side stood soldiers, resting the points of their spears upon the ground. Through my associations with the queen – Queen Victoria, her death and the housekeeper saying to my father 'The worst has happened', the figure of Britannia on a penny, and the twopence which was not enough to buy my father a birthday present – I began telling him of my childhood and of my mother's death. The soldiers' spears reminded me of the soldiers standing by the cross that bore the crucified Christ; of Robinson Crusoe's dream; of a story in our French composition book at school about the inventor of the sewing machine and how he had found the design of the needle an insoluble problem until he had a dream that he was being conducted to the place of execution by soldiers carrying needles as big as spears in which the eye was just above the point, and waking up he knew his problem was solved. I was telling myself in the dream, said Dr Schmid, that the unconscious knew more than the conscious; and this deep knowledge said that the queen had not died, but was on her throne. The dream, he assured me, was a good beginning.

I went to see him once a week. Lying on an old leather couch with a high back, I told him more memories and dreams, sometimes looking at him as he sat quiet behind his desk, like a burly farmer, his right eye watching and encouraging, while his left eye seemed to be looking at the magnolia tree whose branches almost touched the window and to be thinking its own thoughts; and remembering the equation of the left with the unconscious, I wondered what thoughts they were.

I had a dream that I was standing before the temple of Queen Hatshepsut at Deir-el-Bahari, which in the beautiful proportions of its white colonnades stood at the foot of high, tumbling precipices of red rock. I entered, and everything was silent. Before me was a curtained doorway. 'What is behind the curtain?' Dr Schmid asked me. 'A woman,' I answered, 'who is a goddess.'

'What do you want to do?'

'Tear down the curtain.'

116

'What do you feel?'

My voice shook as I replied to my own astonishment, 'Furious anger'. Then I thought: Was that also acted?

After leaving the house that day, as I stood waiting at the tram-stop, I looked across the great field which had been bare stubble when I first came to him and now was green with growing corn. Beyond stood the line of tall trees. 'They are rooted in the earth,' I thought. 'I never thought that before.' And I was happy.

The next time I saw Sonja, I told her of this moment, but to my surprise she wasn't interested. 'Some trees have very deep roots,' she said. How curious women are, I thought. In telling her, I knew that I wanted to give myself to her. Either she had not guessed; or perhaps she wished to tell me that her roots went deeper than mine – and probably, I thought, they do. Or perhaps I was wrong in thinking that she wanted me.

At my unexpected response to Dr Schmid's question I felt that with his help I had broken through to a deep well. But we seemed to get no further. We talked in abstractions. Love, Schmid said, was the reconciliation of individual and collective being. I projected on to Sonja my anima, the image of the secret soul which was not knowable by consciousness, because it was greater than consciousness; and on to me Sonja projected the image of her soul, her animus. Love was individual being because two individuals thus enacted the dialogue and drama of consciousness and the soul. Love was collective being because in the difference of man and woman and in their unity through love the general human soul fulfilled itself. The reconciliation of individual and collective being was made manifest in the child.

Love, as the reconciliation of individual and collective being, said Dr Schmid, should be accepted and revered by society as its creative principle. Sonja had spoken with the true voice of love when she had wished us 'A happy First of August', and out of love I had spoken to the guests: we wanted our love to be one with the collective unity, and that was the sign of our spiritual health. But today love was a prisoner within society's artificial structure of great cities, great states, materialism and machines. Man in society denied the anima

117

and the unconscious. Our society was man's self-murder. Hence the war.

That is not the cause of war, I thought after I had left him. War is not 'man' murdering himself. The states which make war profit by them; it is individuals whom they send to death, and the individuals rebel against the state. If I acquiesce in such ideas, I disown Graeme.

Instead of accepting Schmid's interpretation of my dreams as my bidding myself to acknowledge my soul – he said that I remembered the young girl shouting and leaping at the head of the demonstration in Cairo because she was the image of my soul – I began to dispute with him, using Paul's ideas against him, aware even while I used them that I would not help Paul to establish and make them known. Noting that only the anima of the man, not the animus of the woman, was taken to symbolize the striving of unconscious humanity, I said to Schmid that his ideas were the result of the disintegration of Western culture. The woman as the anima was a substitute for the Virgin Mary as the religious expression of the original cultural unity. That unity having been destroyed by individualism, and the individual having become intellectually weak, he inflated the emotion with which his body provided him into universal mysticism.

I said to Sonja that beneath Schmid's encouraging, paternal calm there was uncertainty. 'How can you say that to me?' she asked quickly. Then she went on: 'I find you so negative. You go round and round people, like a wolf outside a sheepfold, looking for where you can break in.'

As I sat silent, she said to me, 'But you are dear to me, Alick', and took my hand.

When I was home during the vacation, I went one fine Sunday to Hyde Park. At Speakers' Corner, my attention caught by an emphatic, rather thin voice, I joined the small crowd round a speaker on his low wooden box.

'Chlorophyll,' he was saying, 'not money. Chlorophyll maintains the world.' All energy came from the sun. Through photosynthesis this green grass and these trees and the plants and crops in the field made the sun's energy available to man. Blazing up there in the blue sky, the sun was the source of our life. 'You don't live through money,' he said urgently. 'That's

118

what the bankers want you to think. Money only distributes the fruits of life, and because the bankers don't want you to live they keep money short. The real bank is the sun, and money should flow through society like sunlight. Read the writings of the great scientist, Frederick Soddy.'

I went away, impressed. I did what the speaker had said and read the booklets of Frederick Soddy on social credit.

Persuaded of the truth of his ideas, I made them the basis of my criticism of Galsworthy, whom I had chosen as the subject of my weekly lecture. As he was popular and the lectures were open to the people of the town, there was a large audience, and Sonja also came.

I said that *The Man of Property* was a superficial novel because Galsworthy concerned himself only with how attachment to property corrupted its individual owners; far more important was the frustration of all social energy by the very existence of property in the form of money and by the bankers' manipulation of money. In one of the lectures, carried away by my theme, I described the scene in Hyde Park and the sun shining down; and thinking of the war, and of Graeme, I said that there was enough energy in the sun and the earth, and enough knowledge and power in man for us to be able to do all we could imagine; but only if the bankers wanted to use that energy for their own purposes did they make the money and the credit to set it working.

'How they listened to you, Alick!' Sonja said, as we walked away from the University to have supper together at the Storchen Restaurant. When we were sitting over our coffee, she said, 'I think you lecture very much for yourself'. Then she added, 'But you need to know that people are listening to you'. After a silence she asked, 'Do you remember almost the first words you spoke to me?' I recalled how, when she had told me that she taught deaf children, I had said that it must be very solitary to talk and to know that she was not heard. 'Yes,' I answered, and we said no more.

'Would you like me to read Galsworthy too?' Sonja said to me in English; and the sound of her voice made me desire her. 'Yes,' I said.

As we usually did when we came to the Storchen, we looked through the restaurant orchestra's repertoire, of which there was a copy on every table, and chose some Haydn and asked the orchestra to play it for us, and told the waiter to take them some wine. As at the end of the evening I waited for the bill, with my wallet in my hand, Sonja said, 'Will your ideas make everybody rich?' 'Yes, they would,' I said; but I felt the same kind of shock as when she had said, after I had spoken on one of our first evenings together of working with Paul on 'the three realities', 'You believe that will help people?' As I laid a twenty franc note on the plate, Sonja exclaimed, 'I could have given you that dinner for less than a quarter of the price! It's terrible to spend money like this.' Then after a short silence she said, 'But I think you like to act the rich gentleman'.

One Saturday in early November, when the larches were still golden and the sky a clear blue, Sonja and I went for a walk in the hills near the German frontier. In the warm sun we sat on the parapet of a hillside vineyard, spreading out on the flat stones a groundsheet she had brought in her rucksack, and ate the sandwiches she had made. We could see beyond Basle to the hills and on our right stretched the plain of Alsace, patterned with large fields; not far from the foot of the hill clustered the mellow roofs of a small village. The vines were stripped and bare except for a leaf or two of glowing colour, and the weathered grey poles stood in long straight perspectives. Conscious of Sonja at my side, I thought of the vintage and of Dionysus and of my trying to believe that I, the individual artist, gave meaning to all I saw. Now I thought, with a sense of relief, that it was the sun that created with its energy the life of the world, not I, nor the Faustian urge of the culture of the Abendland. In the distance I could see Basle, a pool of building in the softer, hazier landscape. As from a height, I imagined its main streets and massive banks; and, with a momentary stirring of excited hope, I thought that if it was the energy of the sun, liberated by man's labour, that was imprisoned in the banks, then the world was one and I was part of all that was now happening when I felt the beauty of the sunlit earth.

'You are so quiet, Alickchen,' came Sonja's warm voice, and I turned my head and looked into her gently probing eyes. 'I love you,' I said.

With what I felt to be her perverse genius for spoiling a

moment favourable to her, she went on to say that she hadn't understood why in my lectures I had criticized Soames Forsyte's wife, Irene: what was it Galsworthy had done that wasn't right? I said that first, by killing off Irene's lover, Bosinney, Galsworthy had dodged the whole issue of the novel; and then the house designed by Bosinney to glorify art against property he turned into a middle-class residence where Irene, the supposed embodiment of beauty, lived with Jolyon in cultured respectability – or what Nietzsche called 'erbärmliches Behagen'. I heard the edge on my voice which I knew she disliked.

'I don't understand you,' Sonja said. 'Why is it wrong for people to have a nice home and to love one another? Why are you so bitter against them? I'm quite sure it's because of something unconscious in you.'

'Perhaps you're right,' I said; and although I thought she might be, I was resentful.

After one of the lectures, a rather gaunt woman in her late thirties came up to me, and introduced herself as Mrs Burkhardt. She told me how much she was enjoying the lectures, and then shyly said that she and her husband would be very pleased if I would come out one Sunday to their house in the country just outside Basle; and I went the next Sunday. A few weeks later I happened to meet her husband in a beer garden and we drank together, and I asked if I might come out the next Sunday. He said, 'Lily won't be there,' as if he himself had none of the intellectual qualities which I, a university lecturer, must surely seek in my acquaintance; and he spoke with such simplicity that my heart warmed to him. They had two boys, about five and seven years old, with whom I played in the big garden. We went Sunday walks, and after supper I played Haydn duets with Mr Burkhardt and we talked, and I felt at home. I never spoke of Sonja.

I also made the acquaintance of Hans Riemann, a young professor of physics, and the girl he was going to marry. She dressed simply, but extremely well; and with her warm, creamy skin and rather childish, bright lips and orange-golden hair she was very striking. She was consciously the intellectually enlightened girl, but she so enjoyed her looks and her clothes and her intelligence that she was charming. Hans was a Ger-

121

man, with small blue eyes squeezed into little deep holes, and he seemed to feel himself crushed in his muscle-bound bulk – he was well over six feet tall. We became friendly, but never friends. We had talks that stimulated me about science and the impossibility of determining simultaneously the position and the velocity of an atomic particle, which we compared with the illusions of self-knowledge; and Elsa, who was at an art school, taught me to see more in Kandinsky than what I had first called 'fried eggs in nothingness'. But as in the conversations with Frau Heinz and her American friend in the sanatorium, I felt that we were all three concerned with making a good impression. Again, I never spoke of Sonja.

Besides the lectures, I had to take conversation courses at the University. When on the first day of the autumn term I went along the passage to the room where the conversation class was to be held, I heard a loud hum of voices. Entering the room, I found it packed with students, mostly girls. At the consternation on my face – how was I to conduct a conversation course with sixty or seventy people?—there was general laughter. I divided them up into groups which I took in the afternoons at the university, and on one afternoon a week I gave tea to a group in my rooms, so that we should be more at ease and they would talk more freely. Which they did, and the clergyman's widow, who got the tea ready for us, said how pleasant it was to hear in her quiet house the sound of young voices. When they had gone, I missed them, and thought that Sonja kept me from them.

Among those who came to the class in my room, there was a student who was doing a thesis on Galsworthy. He was sitting next me at the tea-table one afternoon, and we talked about social credit. He asked me how I thought the bankers could be compelled to create enough credit to end unemployment, to which I had no answer. In the spring of 1929, at the last class of the term, he asked me if I would like to come with him to a lecture, arranged by a students organization, on the Russian Five Year Plan; and I said that I would.

It was a small meeting. The speaker was a communist, with thin, dead hair and two deeply bitten lines from nose to mouth. He singled me out with his eyes and for a minute on end spoke directly at me. 'The Soviet Five-Year Plan,' he said, 'is the most stupendous event in history.' Nobody, except my father in a religious or moral mood, had I heard speak with such conviction.

Not long afterwards I dropped in at a vegetarian restaurant and looked through the literature hanging on pegs along the wall. There were articles about the virtue of chlorophyll and about a vegetarian diet being the only way in accord with the laws of nature to absorb the energy of the Zoroastrian sun; and there were advertisements of books on social credit. With my mind made uneasy by the student's question and by the speaker on the Five Year Plan, I wondered why particularly in such a setting there should be advertisements for what I had spoken of to Sonja as my new idea.

CHAPTER X

Wondering, when I was at home in Highgate, what I would lecture on in the coming winter, I decided that I would take 'The English Family in Life and Literature'. Looking for books about the family, I found a reference to Friedrich Engels, *The Origin of the Family, Private Property and the State.*

I read it, and also the book to which Engels referred, Lewis Morgan's *Ancient Society.* I was impressed by the moral seriousness of Morgan's style and by the dignity and truthfulness of the Indians, whose society he had studied with such single-mindedness. I liked the tone of respect with which Engels spoke of him, and the simplicity with which Engels said that in writing *The Origin of the Family* he was carrying on as best he could the work of his dead friend, Karl Marx. I read also *The Communist Manifesto* and *Socialism Utopian and Scientific.* I then read Robert Owen's *New Moral World,* and at his wrathful descriptions of private families shut up in boxes I saw the dining-room in Talbot Road and my grandmother with her long curls sitting in the bow window; for though the lace curtains must not be touched, she liked to look through them.

The course of lectures I gave proved popular, and Sonja was always among the large audience. There was no such thing, I said, as the English family. Only the phrase made it seem permanent. In reality, the family was always changing.

Nerving myself to speak his name and that of Marx, I summarized Engels' account of how monogamy arose together with private property. Then, describing the history of the English family, I said that the feudal family of the ruling class, which continued from generation to generation, was founded upon the private ownership of land handed down from father to son. The bourgeois family, which was individual and broke up with the parents' death, and in which the relationship between husband and wife was much more close and personal than in the feudal family, arose with the merchant class and was founded upon private property in money.

Today, I concluded, the English family is 'one of the battlegrounds in the fight between capitalism and socialism'. In the time of Puritanism the family had had a revolutionary function; for through the religious and emotional unity within the individual family the middle class had strengthened itself for the fight against feudalism. After the victory of the middle class, its family life had lost intensity and had become sentimental and comfortable. The middle class could claim no moral sanction for their rule in the name of religion or patriotism, for they believed neither in God nor country. They therefore invested the family with that moral authority to which they had to be able to appeal in order to be able to restrain the individual member of their own class and to keep the working class in subjection. The function of the family ceased to be revolutionary and became conservative.

Sonja began to read *The Origin of the Family,* but didn't finish it. Engels was a superficial extrovert, she said. Some people married for money but marriage still came out of love and no woman bore a child to hand on private property. I defended Engels, but felt that my defence was forced and insincere. For I wrote home regularly because I was held in the relationship of father and son; and I wanted at moments to marry Sonja. The bourgeois character of the family as an institution was the cause neither of that desire nor of the sense of belonging to the family of my childhood. Only if I denied my own feelings could I defend Engels. I remembered how David had said to me in Ruhleben that even if Germany and England were fighting for markets, the men in the trenches were fighting because they loved their country. States and politicians exploited that love for their own profit, and the bourgeois institution of marriage misused sexual love to maintain private property; but love was nonetheless real. Yet not to defend Engels was to side with his bourgeois enemies. It was to capitulate to the family, to the inert, comfortable, dishonest institution which was a mainstay of capitalism against socialism. That a man and woman married out of love did not change the fact that they were made husband and wife only by the authority of the bourgeois state; to marry was to recognize the state.

Sonja also said that Engels without knowing it wrote of marriage as a man, unaware of what the man's unconsciousness asked of the woman; and thereby she was telling me, I knew,

125

that I was unaware of what I asked of her. I asked her to come and hear me say in public how deep in the time of Cromwell was the love between husband and wife, and hear me quote, as if I were speaking the words to her, from Cromwell's letters to his wife: 'I have nothing to tell thee, yet indeed I love to write to my Dear who is very much in my heart'. Then after the lecture I found her waiting for me alone in the street and we went to have dinner together at the Storchen. I knew that she was waiting for me to speak. I had said in my lecture that the family of the 19th century was being undermined by the disappearance of the individual private business, the rise of the working class and the emancipation of women, and that the movement today was towards a new kind of family which would be fused into society as a whole. I knew that now she wanted me to talk, not in abstract generalities, but about ourselves, and that in her mind was still what she had said when we came back from Lake Constance. But I asked her what she thought of the lecture, needing her praise. 'Good,' she said. 'Good.'

During the winter and spring of the following year, 1930, I saw a good deal of Hans Riemann and Elsa, generally meeting them in a café. Hans said one day that he would like to work with me, as he knew nobody else who had thought so much about the revolution. But I didn't respond.

I said, however, that it was necessary to apply Marxism to Marx. The materialist conception of history which said that the social superstructure was determined by the economic basis, was itself determined by the economic conditions in which it had been conceived. The economic factor was made into the primary cause of historical movement because the decisive development at the time when Marx and Engels were writing was the economic fact of the industrial revolution; and so they wrote as they did, without knowing why. But now that the material basis of the new collective society had been completed, it was no longer economic facts which were significant, but Paul's question whether a collective society could have cultural content.

Hans and Elsa agreed. Making sweeping, abrupt cuts with his forearm, while his small eyes snapped, Hans said that all mechanical determinism was absolutely finished; and Elsa,

126

speaking in her light voice and looking at me with such attractive gravity that I wanted to smile, said that Marxism was antiquated realism and it should learn from abstract art to see reality as the ambivalent relation of perspectives. 'That would be an idea for a picture, Hans!' she said excitedly. 'An infinitely alternatingly outwards-inwards cone of Marxism being applied to Marxism being applied to Marxism!' Then we all three talked of Freud and Jung, and the possible unconscious motives of socialism; and in the silences when each of us was thinking of something more to say, and I turned the delicate coffee-cup and Hans kneaded the tablecloth, I thought that I should have got up and gone away.

During the winter Sonja and I had once or twice gone ski-ing, and at the end of the winter I again had a haemorrhage. It didn't alarm me nor excite me with the prospect of escaping into the snows, but I went to a doctor. A girl showed me into the waiting-room, and I had an impulse I barely resisted to kiss her. The doctor found nothing much wrong, and I soon forgot.

My birthday was approaching, when I should be at the *mezzo del cammin di nostra vita*. Sonja prepared a feast in her room, and a few days later she took me to Mozart's *The Magic Flute*. I remembered how I had first asked her to come to the theatre, and thereby had in reality been asking her to marry me.

Moved so deeply by Pamina's aria that I took Sonja's hand, which she gave lovingly, I thought: I am again saying 'Marry me', and I have no right to hold her hand.

It is terrible, I thought, to be so incapable of truth. I am neither the one thing nor the other. I yield to the emotion which makes me want to give myself in marriage, and to avoid the act I call it recognition of the state. And here in my usual restaurant my solitary dinner is brought to me by a waitress for money, and I say to myself like Bloom, *un homme moyen sensuel* of middle age, 'Eating is real' and sit over my café kirsch and read the *Daily Mail* I have bought at the station bookstall. 'Can a man,' asked Parolles, 'know what he is and be what he is?' The answer, it seemed, was 'Yes'.

When I was in England for the vacation, I stayed for some days with my brother, who for some years now had been pro-

127

fessor of anatomy at a Welsh university. Their daughter was almost four years old, very like Constance at the same age, and they were both very proud of her.

We looked at an album of father's photographs of us as children; and as we talked about our fears of him, I felt how strong was the bond between us, even while I was thinking that he, having become himself a father, had gone over to father's side. And so I resisted his friendly urgings not to be content with a salary of £120 a year and the additional hundred pounds or so I made from private lessons. 'Remember,' he said; 'you are getting on.'

At home, there was grief and depression. One morning in the early summer, my stepmother was seated in front of her dressing-table brushing her hair, when my father heard her give a little choking noise, and looking round he saw her collapsed in her chair. She recovered, but her speech remained disturbed; and though she could slowly move about, when she sat down she seemed to huddle her head into her shoulders, as if in anticipation of a blow. She fumbled with shapeless sentences like a person trying to pick something up with numbed fingers. She confused pronouns, and time and money, and called our neighbours by our name; and as they had young sons and daughters, I wondered whether it was her own longing for children and a real family that had broken through her mind.

Yet behind the heavy inarticulacy she was her old self, and she conveyed to me that, while others could only watch her in helpless incomprehension, I, the poet with the divine spark, could understand her. But in fact it was my father who understood her, with that knowledge given, I thought, by years of living together, bearing what he could not change.

Taking it easy, for my father's leg pained him if he tried to go his old pace, he and I sometimes made the round down Hampstead Lane and back over Parliament Fields; and one afternoon we visited the eighteenth century house at Kenwood, and my father gave me a Devonshire cream tea in the converted stables. Both of us, I felt, were conscious of the years; but though we knew the past was gone, at moments the pain and hardness left my father's eyes, and they became deep and sweet as we talked together.

128

As we sat on over our tea, I felt impelled to speak to him of Sonja. He asked me if we loved each other, and I answered that we did. 'Then if you have said so, you owe it to her to marry her.' I didn't answer, and he said brusquely, 'Don't swither'.

An echo of our old quarrel arose when in another talk my father spoke of the loss of income he had suffered since the Wall Street crash in 1929, and said that Britain would never recover until the workers put their backs into it. When I began to argue that there was no unemployment in Russia and that the unemployment here was due to the system, he cut me short, saying, 'I don't think you understand what you're talking about, my boy'.

That was the tone in which he had spoken to me when I came back from Ruhleben, and in which he had said also of Graeme that he didn't understand what he was saying. In the bottom shelf of the bookcase in the dining-room, which now served my father as his study, was the black-japanned deed-box, with A.B.W. painted on it in bold white letters, where, I imagined, my father kept his will and his copy of Graeme's book, which, if he could, he would have suppressed; and the deed-box was locked and padlocked. Against whom? Engels, I thought, was right: within the bourgeois family are all the contradictions of bourgeois society.

Sonja and I turned a corner into a short street, down each side of which were shops displaying postcards, ornamental wooden boxes and trays and spoons, Alpine walking-sticks, Catholic images. At the end, warmed red stone like the Münster at Basle, rose the west front of Strasbourg Cathedral.

It was only a couple of hours since we had met. After a lunch in the hotel we had gone up to our room, and I had given her the presents I had brought—a bottle of Houbigant perfume and an old Chinese embroidered jacket. She had kissed me, and with a smile of shy self-consciousness she had put a few drops of the scent behind her ears and slipped on the jacket. 'It's too beautiful for me,' she said, as she looked at herself in the tall glass. She took it off again, and said we must go out.

I asked Sonja to stop, and we stood on the pavement and looked at the cathedral; and as we then moved down the street,

I still kept my eyes on it. In the porch we bought a book about its architecture, and went in.

The choir was empty, and there were only a few visitors. We sat down on two rush-bottomed chairs in the nave, and looked, and whispered to each other. Then I began to read the book, and after a little time Sonja rose quietly and went away.

I stopped reading. I looked towards the still mysterious altar and up into the vaulted roof. I felt space separated from the world of streets and shops outside; and being the architecture of a cathedral of God, it had meaning that I knew.

I saw Sonja, in her dark brown coat trimmed with fur, with a deep orange scarf at the neck, slowly walking down the north aisle and then stop to look at a carved tomb.

I remembered Napoleon's words in the cathedral of Chartres: 'Un athée serait mal à l'aise ici'. I was not uneasy, but passive.

Sonja came up behind me. 'May I have the book?' she said. And taking it, she said with a smile, 'You'll come soon?' I responded to her smile, and when she had gone I felt peaceful. Why should I not be?

I got up and found Sonja. 'Come and look at the Pillar of the Angels', she said.

We reserved a table in a quiet corner of a good restaurant, and drank a fine Riesling with our dinner. As we were having coffee, I said it was three years to the day since the first time I had returned from England, so I had brought something else for her; and I put my hand in my breast pocket for my wallet.

'So you remember the exact day,' Sonja said. 'You are very dependent on outward occasion.'

That was a shock to me. I wondered why I had spoken of the anniversary, which had been so soon after the time when she had broken down, and felt a kind of jealousy of this stronger woman who knew me.

I took out of my wallet an envelope in which, wrapped in tissue paper was a small square of vellum, cut from a medieval missal, with an illuminated initial on a gold background. Sonja unwrapped it, and laid it carefully on her palm, and looked at it without speaking.

'Did you choose this on purpose, Alick?' she asked.

'How do you mean?' I asked.

She held it out to me. The initial I had chosen was 'I'.

'It was the nicest they had,' I said.

Arm in arm, we went back to the hotel.

When we were making love, I said, 'Shall we get married?' For a long moment Sonja did not speak. Then she said, 'Did you say that with full consciousness?' 'No,' I answered. 'That was what I thought. We'll forget that you said it.'

CHAPTER XI

I came back to my rooms in Basle.

The University term was soon beginning, and there was still a good deal of work to do on my lectures, which were to be on Walter Pater and Oscar Wilde.

The Bavarian servant girl brought me my breakfast, and I listened to her singing as she worked in the kitchen. The clergyman's widow came to clear away and gossip. As I sat at my desk by the window all morning, across the privet hedge I saw the postman with his brown satchel, the milkman's jingling cart, the dustman on Tuesdays and Fridays; and just before twelve o'clock outside the school on the other side of the road the mothers came and stood waiting and chatting at the foot of the steps, and then there was a torrent of children and a noise like a burst of sunlight.

I walked down for my lunch to the tea-room where I had met Sonja, the streets full of bicycles and crowded trams and clerks and shop-girls on their way home for their mid-day meal; and Sonja and I in Strasbourg Cathedral seemed to have been in a different world than this life.

I came back at night from the restaurant, or from my risotto milanese in the renowned railway station buffet; or from an evening with the Riemanns, now married. The streets were dark and empty, the windows of the private families lit and curtained, the school-block dead and black like a pyramid. Sometimes this presence of darkness and dead stillness seemed nearer to me than the daytime and the public streets, as if it were the authoritative presence watching me in my own mind when I thought of myself and Sonja and came to no conclusion.

Then I went through to my bedroom at the back, and snuggled down in bed; and conscious of a malicious, solitary satisfaction, I wondered against whom I felt it.

One morning I woke up soon after dawn, and outside the window was a shining mountain of crystal quartz, veined with black. That was the work of a witch in the night. The next instant the crystal veined mountain was the boughs and twigs of a leafless tree against the white morning sky, and a thrush began singing. 'I shall remember this,' I thought.

It was November and Sonja's birthday was coming near. She had done what she had said: she made not even an allusion to Strasbourg. I had not gone to her flat. She came to my lectures, and we had supper together afterwards; and because the evening had passed and nothing had happened when she said goodbye to me with her eyes averted and her lips drawn back hard against her upper teeth, I preferred to think that she was bearing it.

But for her birthday, though it would be again proving my dependence on outward occasion, I would have to go to her. When I said that we must celebrate, she asked me if I would like to come.

What should I bring her? I thought of a ring, but 'No, I can't'. I brought her a brooch of garnets and pearls. When after supper I put into her hand the small box, I knew what I had not wanted to know: she would think it was a ring. She opened it, and when she saw the brooch, she let herself fall on the divan and cried heartbreakingly. When she began to be hysterical, I took her by the nape of the neck and shook her. 'I'll go mad again,' she said. We cleared the supper-table, and washed up. 'That's how it is,' she said, as she was putting away the things. 'No man marries a girl like me.'

As I walked home across the Rhine, I thought, 'I secure my calm through her suffering. It is pleasant, as Lucretius said, to stand in safety upon the land and watch a ship in the storm'.

Not long afterwards she rang up and asked me to come to her again. I went; and we seemed to go on as we had before I had spoken of marriage.

Towards the end of the year Sonja decided to move into a flat in a new block in Little Basle. Paul came down to stay with me over Christmas and the New Year, and the three of us went round the antique shops, Paul advising Sonja what carpets to buy for her larger rooms.

This was the first time that Paul and Sonja had met. Within an hour he seemed to know her better than I did; and it was I who was the third person. I left Sonja unsatisfied, I thought, because I liked to overlay antagonism with an abstract emotion of love and deny the reality of my feelings until, as at Stras-

133

bourg, I yielded and then drew back again. When she and I were trying to be happy, I made her, because of all that was unspoken, behave like a child. But at every moment Paul challenged and attacked, and she could meet him as a woman.

After choosing the carpets, we went to a café to meet Hans and Elsa. They knew Paul well from hearsay, because I had spoken of 'the three realities', and presently Elsa asked him when the great work was to be finished, to which Paul involuntarily, I thought, glancing at me, made some joking reply. Because he and Sonja were there, the tone among us was different from when Hans and Elsa and I talked together. Sonja and I said little, while the three of them talked of Germany, and Hans vehemently denied that science was the expression of Western culture, which, he said, was the myth of the German National Socialist Party.

One day in the early part of this year, 1931, a clergyman came, unannounced, to see me. He said that he was from the Missionschule, of which Sonja's father had once been in charge. I had been most warmly recommended to him, he said, as a teacher of English, and he wished to offer me the post of director of English teaching at the school. It would only mean fifteen hours a week, which I could well combine with my work at the University, and it would give me an assured income and position. He earnestly hoped that I would consider the offer. My pupils would take up missionary work in Africa.

I can't make my money, I thought, teaching men English so that they can preach Christianity. Also it would cut my summer freedom from three months to seven weeks. I refused

I told Sonja of the offer and of the moral reason for refusing it. 'You must do what you think right,' she said. But when I told her of Lenin's phrase for clergymen – 'policemen in surplices' – she said that it was unjust. The Basle missionaries helped the Africans to a better life, they gave them hospitals and schools, and showed them how to grow more food. Hospitals or no hospitals, I said, missionaries are there to make the people quiet with Christianity. 'But your father was a missionary,' she said; and I had the misgiving that my pleasure in Lenin's phrase, like my pleasure in *The Origin of the Family*, was a betrayal.

'Policemen' – when I met Dr Oettinger in the tea-room, I

thought that the state prosecutor was kind to Sonja as I was not. Then I remembered the evening at his house, and how the telephone call about Sacco and Vanzetti had changed him; and about this time I had to be interpreter at the judicial examination of an uneducated English girl suspected of having caused the death of her illegitimate baby which she had come to Basle to have in secret, letting her Cook's party go back to England without her, and I was shocked as I watched the assistant state prosecutor, with whom I had the discussion about the supposedly Freudian film, use his interrogating technique upon her and then contemptuously dismiss her.

On the afternoon of May 1st I went down to the Marktplatz. I was going for the first time to the celebration of May Day; and in the preface to the *Condition of the English Working Class,* from which I had quoted in my lectures on the English family, Engels had written after the great May Day demonstration in Hyde Park, four years before I was born, 'Glad and proud I am to have lived to see this day'.

There were many people standing about, though not so many that I could not move among them freely; and in the brightness of the afternoon there was less expectancy than when the packed crowd waited in the darkness of Carneval morning and the drumming grew louder from the sidestreets. 'They are coming,' I heard somebody say near me, and the head of the column appeared in the curve of the street that led into the square from the bridge over the Rhine. I made my way over to that corner, and watched them come in, rank after rank, shouting. The pace gained a quick and firm beat as there came a band of fifes and drums, behind which followed a company of young girls in blue blouses, singing as they marched:

> Denn was wir singen
> Heisst Klassenkampf!

In their high, ringing voices, 'Klassenkampf' cut like the edge of a sword, as I stood among the onlookers.

I moved about among the crowd. One of the girls in a blue blouse came up to me with a tray of red rosettes. She held one out to me. 'Wollen Sie ein Mai-Bänderli?' 'Nein,' I said, and turned away.

I went back to my rooms. The house was quiet, and every-

135

body seemed to be out. As if all my vitality had left me with the shock of hearing myself say 'Nein', I lay down on the sofa, put Sonja's cushion on the arm where it would come under the nape of my neck, and went to sleep.

Sonja and I went out for a long day in the country, and in the early evening above the village of St Ursanne we sat under a hedge beside a hayfield ready for cutting, while the bells rang for Sunday service. Why am I sitting here, I thought, with her, when reality is movement and change? But so is the ringing of the bells. No culture but ours has ever filled the evening with such innocent and heart-breaking peace, while Sonja sits beside me and waits for me to speak.

Because I could find no decision in my consciousness, I thought one night that I would try the *Sortes Virgilianae*.

I had been working on my lectures, to which I had given the title '*Hamlet* and *Ulysses*'. My professor had asked, when I submitted the title, what the two works had to do with each other, and I quoted Stephen Dedalus: '(*Tapping his forehead*) It is here that I must kill the priest and the king'. Shakespeare, I was saying in the course, could make Hamlet kill the king because soon the King of England was to be beheaded; but Joyce couldn't recognise that his priest and king today was capitalism. Therefore Stephen only broke the lamp in a brothel and got himself knocked down by a brick-faced English Tommy.

This evening I suddenly thought: Supposing I turn the sentence round? Not: in order to kill the priest and the king, it is necessary to destroy capitalism. But: in order to destroy capitalism, it is necessary to kill the priest and the king. What would that mean?

I tried my associations to 'priest and king'. My father, the Kaiser, the doctors in the sanatorium, bankers and money, Paul, West European culture, Zarathustra, David and the young lad leaning against the tree who said, 'I have jumped a step and that is what no step forgives me'; the stone in the ground which had obsessed me in the mountains. Then came the figure of Dr Schmid as priest, the goddess behind the veil, Sonja in Strasbourg Cathedral. I tried associations with killing, and thought of the boy I had pushed down the slope at school, of myself as Blifil, and of 'Each man kills the thing he loves'. Then I asked, 'Whom do I feel like when I kill?' and to my surprise I thought of myself having my dinner in the restaurant, saying to myself, 'Eating is real'.

Was my real desire to produce chaos and annihilate all values so as to live the live of *l'homme moyen sensuel*? Or was my impotence before the unreason of my associations the contemporary form of awe before the priest and the king? Must that awe be overcome in order to be free from capitalism?

But if I said that this awe before the unconscious must be overcome, would I not be denying the truth I had learned in that moment of 'furious anger' and in the succeeding recognition that trees are rooted in the earth? Would I not also be denying that awe and that truth if I held back from marrying Sonja? Or if I did marry her, would I be surrendering to priest and king, and so upholding capitalism?

Then I remembered the *Sortes Virgilianae*.

My stepmother had given me an eighteenth century French edition of Virgil, a small duodecimo volume bound in leather with fine gold tooling. I knew exactly where it was in the bookcase, and went to the place and took it out. Looking upwards, I opened it, and then lowering my head and shutting my eyes I put my finger on the left-hand page, about a third of the way down. I opened my eyes and removed my finger. The word beneath it was 'conjunx'.

It was in line 620 of the fourth book of the *Aeneid*:

Fit Beroë, Tmarii conjunx longaeva Dorycli.

I noticed that *Beroë*, if the order of the syllables was reversed, was like Sonja's surname, Huber; and *Fit* could be taken as English: she would be a fit wife.

Then I thought I had better look at the context. I found that this *conjunx* was a false appearance. She was not Beroë, but Iris, who, at the bidding of Juno, had taken on the form of Beroë in order to come among the Trojan women and persuade them to burn the ships and so prevent the Trojans from reaching Italy and founding Rome. So was I being told that if I married her, she would hold me back from reaching my Italy? The uncertainty of interpretation, I thought, was comic.

I also felt it not comic at all that I should read and talk of Marxism and yet believe that some power had made my finger light upon that word – *conjunx*.

137

I went to see Dr Schmid again and persuaded myself that there was serious meaning in his words when he said that he also at times felt himself estranged from 'universal happening', and that in order to become one with it again he went out into his garden and lay down upon the compost heap. And after he had spoken of the wisdom of China, I drew thin, smooth sticks from his hand, and then we consulted the German translation of a Chinese work to find the symbol to which the number of sticks I had drawn corresponded; mystic sayings then opened the symbol, and if I listened in sincerity they would show me my road.

Late one night I wrote to Sonja and asked her to marry me, fastened down the envelope, addressed it, stamped it and went out to the post-box. It was a fine, warm night, and the lime-trees were in blossom. Their branches overhung the post-box on the wall, and the light of a street lamp, round which a moth circled, shone through the green leaves. I lifted the flap of the post-box and held the letter in the opening. Then I drew it out again and went back, my steps loud on the pavement. I thought of my brother going out at midnight before he returned to France for the last time. His choice between serving the state or defying its power I did not even set before myself.

While I was home for the vacation, the National Government was formed. Every Sunday evening during the summer I had been giving English lessons to the German Consul in Basle and to two of his friends, men of about my own age, lecturers at the University – or rather, I was paid to sit at table with them and eat the exquisite dinners prepared by the Consul's cook, and then to listen to their English conversation in the effeminately furnished drawing-room, the Consul outstretched in a deep arm-chair and playing with his monocle. In the spring the conversation had been about University intrigues and Basle society scandals, intermixed with pseudo-psychological discussion that often seemed to be nosing its way towards obscenity; but in the summer, when a financial crisis broke in Austria, it became political. The financial crisis hit Germany, one of the biggest banks suspended payments, and the Consul began to be distraught. Once he was called away to the telephone, and returned wringing his manicured hands and repeating 'My poor country, my poor country'.

138

In England, among the advertisements on the hoardings, there were posters that proclaimed in great letters 'The New Party' and called for support from all who wanted action and an end to talk. Day after day the newspaper placards announced further losses of gold, further falls in the pound, rumours of a moratorium, hopes of loans from France and the United States to tide Britain over. I had never seen my father so concerned and anxious; even when I came home after the war he still had not completely lost the confidence I remembered from our childhood that the folly of governments could not disturb our security and that all their wisdom was what we already knew. But now, when on the fine late summer mornings we went out on to the terrace to smoke an after-breakfast cigarette, the sun shining on the mellow brick wall of the long garden where my father would presently go and work, he would sit in brooding silence and then shake his head, and say, 'Things can't go on like this'. He used to bring out his big ledger and spread many papers on the dining-room table, and speak to nobody. But it was not so much any fall in the value of his investments that troubled him as the collapse of the pound itself – it was his loyal faith in it that had made me handle with awe the first golden sovereign he had given me. We had my stepmother's sister staying with us, the aunt with whom I had spent Sundays when I was at Trinity College, Dublin, and as we drank our coffee in the drawing-room after dinner she encouraged my father to lay the blame on the workers. 'Two million loafing on the dole,' she said; 'no wonder the budget doesn't balance.' And my stepmother, dumb and sunk in her chair, listened with a glowering sadness in her eyes. Then Auntie May would go to the piano round which we had once sung our Sunday hymns, place her rings beside the last treble notes, and play Beethoven, and my stepmother would beat time, gently caressing the air.

I bought the programme of the New Party – 'A National Policy, advanced by Sir Oswald Mosley', and discussed it with Paul, who was on a visit to his parents. Though I had been reading Marxism for some time, I had examined by it my own living rather than the world around me. When I now read on the first page of the pamphlet that 'the position of the industrialist becomes daily more impossible and that of the workers daily more precarious', I thought, 'He writes as if he wanted to help both sides'. So when Paul suggested that we should get in touch with the New Party, since 'the three realities' provided the cultural basis which their policy lacked, I didn't respond.

When the National Government was formed towards the end of August, my father was at first hopeful that things would now get better. But the drain on the pound continued, and when the *Morning Post* announced that Britain had gone off the gold standard, there was a gloom over the breakfast table as if the King had died. Before I left for Basle, Parliament had been dissolved and the election campaign had begun.

I hated the great posters along the hoardings 'Let the doctor do his job', 'Your savings aren't safe with Labour'. I felt this hectoring National Government to be my enemy like the Immigration Officer at Dover who knew the secrets of men's hearts. But I said nothing when my father and my stepmother's sister approved the *Morning Post* and my stepmother's eyes besought me to keep silent.

I had been in town, buying books on Chartism in preparation for the winter lectures on Dickens and Thackeray, and was walking up the east side of Bedford Square into Gower Street, when a little way ahead I saw the backs of people standing still on a corner and cars halted in the roadway. I heard shouting, repeated, and could distinguish 'Down with the National Government!'; and I could see, jerkily moving across Gower Street to the right, red banners. Then between the heads of the people watching I saw the faces of workers, some in caps, some bare-headed, and beside them, every few yards, walked a policeman. They passed, and I looked after the loose end of the procession. I remembered the girls in their blue shirts wheeling on to the Marktplatz and their high voices singing. These marchers in a London street, they are Klassenkampf; and as I went on between the unbroken fronts of Georgian houses, the long vista leading to the heights of Highgate and the hazy spire, I imagined them still marching.

On the other side of the earth, the Japanese began their attack on Manchuria, and the *Morning Post* said to the League of Nations 'Don't interfere'. In the whole world was disturbance.

When I got back to Basle Sonja was away. She was staying

with her married sister, to whose baby daughter she was god-mother.

On the hills above the lake of Biel, some sixty miles from Basle, Dr Schmid had built a small log cabin in the woods where, as he said to me, he used to go when he wanted to be alone. His wife was never allowed to come there, but he had told Sonja that he would let us have it for a week-end, and in a few days time I was to meet her at the nearest railway station.

The night before our meeting I spent in a hotel at Biel, and early in the morning, with my rucksack on my back, set out on the twenty mile walk.

It was a lovely clear autumn day and soon I had climbed high enough into the hills for my eyes to take in almost the whole length of the lake beneath the morning sun. I remembered following a winding path above the Mediterranean when I had gone down from Berlin to spend Christmas with my father and stepmother who were wintering on the Riviera, and thinking that Nietzsche would often have seen the same sight. Then one evening in the pension where my father and step-mother were staying, a Jewish girl had told our fortunes. When she came to me, she looked at my hand for what seemed a long time, and then she said, 'You are not independent. Not really.' I knew that it was true, but would not admit it.

We met, and in the village shop bought food for the week-end, Sonja reading out from her list in a happy voice, yet with nervousness in her laugh.

We walked out of the village, and consulting the sketch map which Dr Schmid had given to Sonja, we followed a footpath across fields into a wood. On the further fringe of it, on the edge of a hill looking across the lake, stood the cabin made of pine logs. 'Here is the tree!' cried Sonja, and putting her hand into a hole in the trunk she drew out a key.

We unpacked the food and settled in. Before Sonja started to make the supper, we walked out from among the trees and across the grass in the evening sunlight to a stone wall. Beyond it, the ground fell gently to the lake, whose calm water under the clear sky still held the memory of the day. Hand in hand, we stood and looked. 'It is beautiful,' said Sonja. The church in the village struck the hour and the peaceful quiet deepened. Sonja caressed my hand with her warm fingers, and when I turned my head towards her, the light and power in her grey-blue eyes consumed me. After a moment, I asked her to marry me. 'I don't know, Alick,' she said.

When we had finished supper, she took my box of cigarettes, and tearing off the lid she wrote on the inside of it 'Ja', and the date and her name 'Sonja', and gave it me.

When I woke next morning, Sonja lying beside me still asleep, I remembered, and felt no joy. After breakfast we went for a walk along rough lanes, rather slowly, because Sonja's feet, as often, were paining her. As she hung upon my arm, she talked about how she would arrange her flat so that we could live there, and how we could manage on my university salary and money from lessons and the income from my capital. I listened and answered. When we returned and Dr Schmid's cottage was visible among the trees I thought that it was in submission to him that I had asked Sonja to marry me. But I have said that I will marry, and I must not change.

After we had eaten our lunch, cooked on a wood fire, Sonja showed me photographs from her stay with her sister, some of them of herself with the young baby. As I took them, one by one, and she talked about them, it went through my mind that we had not spoken of having children; and though it seemed as if Sonja were showing me the photographs because she wanted us to have children, yet I doubted it.

I began to speak about my time at home, the formation of the National Government, and the hypocritical use of the word 'national'. Sonja interrupted, and asked whether on our walk that morning she had talked too much about the flat. I went on and told her about the marchers with the red flags, shouting against the National Government, and said that I had felt that I should be with them. 'Du bist viel zu zart dazu,' she said – you are far too delicate and slight and tender-minded for that; 'unless', she added, 'you became a fanatic'. That is a possibility, I thought, but not likely, because of the kind of happiness I enjoy. We should rather, Sonja went on, work on ourselves, so that we could help each other as only a man and a woman could.

That night as we lay in bed, around us the utter silence of the wood, she asked me, 'You will always love me, Alick, won't you?' 'I don't know. How can anybody know?' I answered.

142

'Do you mean that perhaps you won't be faithful to me?' she asked. 'I don't know,' I replied. 'Then why did you ask me to marry you?' I made no answer and Sonja burst into tears.

We went back to Basle next day, I having said that I would 'think about it'.

CHAPTER XII

The strain was different from the time after Strasbourg. We saw each other once or twice a fortnight. She would call at my rooms between morning and afternoon school, and we would go and have lunch; or we would meet after my lecture for supper in a restaurant. She was calmer, as though, whatever happened, she had a place of refuge and knew that her strength of resolve was greater than mine.

Only once, on her birthday, she broke down. She had asked me to her flat, and I had brought her a Chinese vase. After she had looked at it and placed it on the table, she said with hostility in her eyes, 'Your friend Paul made you like Chinese things.' Later in the evening she said, 'This is the fifth birthday you have come to me. I have given you five years while you have stayed in your room with your Frau Pfarrer and had her as a mother you needn't love.' Then she began to cry. But except on that one evening she spoke about me quietly, relating what she had thought when she was alone, as though she felt bound not to withhold from me what would help me, if only I would listen.

There was one evening in her flat when we had made love and had been almost happy, though there was a tone of bitterness in Sonja's voice when she said from the bed, as I stood, before dressing again, in front of the long mirror, 'Your boy's body you are so proud of'. The mood changed as we were finishing supper and I began to talk about the unemployment in England and a conversation I had had with Hans about Hitler. Sonja made brief remarks, and then she said in a sad voice, 'You have gone away again. You can't stand nearness. You always think as if you were alone. You should think with love, but you won't.'

When I talked again of the march of the workers in London and of my feeling that I was standing aside, she said, 'Your Communism, as you call it, isn't your real self. You drive yourself into it because you are afraid of living.'

I answered her that whatever the motives of my interest, the truth of communism was not thereby affected.

144

I said to myself that what was happening in the world, was happening. I had seen a newsreel of the Japanese bombing of the open city of Shanghai, and photographs of a row of bodies, mutilated, twisted, and charred. They recalled that stump of an arm, with the hacked, protruding bone, that the beggar had thrust up into the square of my window as the train stopped at the wayside station in Egypt. Sonja, when she reproached me with being afraid of living, wanted me to forget that this was the reality of living, and always had been. The world in which I had believed when at home on a summer evening I had heard the band on Parliament Fields play 'God Save the King' and had stood up from my chair to attention, had never existed.

I met Dr Oettinger at lunch in the tea-rooms, and the talk turned to Manchuria and the bombing of Shanghai. When I said that Japan should be brought before the League of Nations and charged with inhumanity, Dr Oettinger shook his head. 'Politics are politics, dear Herr West,' he said. 'Morality is the comfort and entertainment of the unhappy individual. Leave good and evil for him.' And when I talked with the Burkhardts one Sunday evening, she was on my side, but he opposed us both, with a hard intolerance in his voice, as he said that private people should obey their own country's laws; if they presumed to tell other states what to do and what not to do, there would be an end of government. I heard my father's tone, and I thought that the government and authority they both wished to preserve was that which the bourgeoisie with its conservative morality of the family defended against socialism. As I heard the accent in Sonja's voice of good Basle society, I thought that she was on their side when she said that my interest in communism was not my real self.

Yet when during the week of Carneval Sonja had to take her class to a children's home in the mountains and gave me her key in case during her absence, as she said, fire broke out in her flat, every day, under a compulsion I could not resist, I went to her flat.

Everywhere it was scrupulously tidy, and there was the same fragrance of cleanliness as at home. I opened the windows and dusted in the sitting-room and her bedroom. I opened her peasant-art wardrobe, painted with wild flowers on a light-blue ground, and in the dark was the row of familiar dresses on their hangers. I stood in the middle of the bright kitchen and looked round, and turned on the gas of the stove and then turned it off again. Reluctantly I left, and stood at the top of the stone stairs. It is like me, I thought: when the flat is empty, when she is not here and it is therefore safe, I come secretly.

Early this year, out of motives I refrained from examining, I started a savings account at the People's Bank, and was given a money-box with openings for twenty and fifty centime, one franc and two franc pieces. I kept it in a pigeon-hole in my desk, and looked at it and took it down from time to time while I was working, and I also looked at the column of entries in my savings book, slowly lengthening as I took the box to the bank to be opened with a key I didn't have.

One morning in April Sonja rang up and told me that Dr Schmid had died. A small cut had set up blood-poisoning and in four days he was dead.

I feared the effect of his death upon her. When, however, that same day she came to see me, she was calm; but it seemed to me that there was a greater distance between us.

I saw her more often during the next two or three weeks, and the sense of distance grew stronger. It was as if a third person had left the room, and we were now left alone and had nothing to say to each other.

I thought that for nearly five years we had been supposed to love each other, but that perhaps the bond between us had been what Dr Oettinger on the first day I had seen her had called her 'difficulties' and my desire to displace Schmid. Now Schmid was dead: she seemed to be with him in her thoughts, and from me was lifted the pressure of his bidding not to deny my soul. Yet still at moments her face seemed to me to be transfigured.

Remembering such a moment when I was alone, I thought that it was flattering self-deception to tell myself that if I left her I should be killing my soul. Actually, I should fall in love again.

There was a young girl, Claire Endrich, who came to my phonetics class at the University. I used to stand by each student in turn, closing my eyes so as to listen with greater concentration to their repeating of the sentences after me. When I came to this girl and listened and then opened my eyes again, hers challenged me.

In June, on a fine Sunday morning, Sonja and I went out to spend the day on the banks of the Rhine in Alsace. We returned in the evening to her flat.

All day there had been a distance between us. After supper, we talked and waited, until the distance became hopeless.

'You won't marry me, will you,' Sonja said.

This is the end, I thought.

'No,' I answered.

'You had better go now.' She got up, and we went into the small hall. 'Goodbye, Alick,' she said, and opened the door for me to go. When I was standing outside, just as she was closing the door, she made the gap wider again, and said, her face beautiful and her voice calm, 'Du hast nicht die Kraft gehabt, das zu tun was Du hättest tun sollen' – You have not had the strength to do what you ought to have done. Then the closed door was before my face.

I was walking down the street to the bridge across the Rhine. A clock jutted out above a shop, and the time was ten minutes to twelve. Another hundred yards there was another clock, showing the same time. At the sight of the large black hands on the white face inexplicable fear, and knowledge, closed round my heart.

The next day I rang up, but each time there was no reply. On the Tuesday morning I was working when I was called to the telephone. Out of the dark came Dr Oettinger's voice, saying that he had heavy news for me, and asking me to come to him at his house. He told me what I already knew.

That evening I went out to the place under the flowering acacia trees beside the Rhine where we had been on Sunday, and watched the flowing water. The next day I went to her flat, where on the writing table was laid out, neatly ticketed, what she wanted her relatives and friends to have; for me, Herr West, there were the Haydn duets, the Chinese vase and the brooch, and whatever else I had given her, and rolled up underneath the table the Persian carpet for her bedside.

Out of consideration for me, Dr Oettinger arranged that there should not be an inquest In three days she was to be cremated, in accordance with the wish in her letter to him. I

147

could not stay in Basle, but must go away till the eve of the funeral. I went to Strasbourg.

As I came near the corner of the street, 'This,' I thought, 'is what Freud would call obedience by delayed action'. My heart was thumping as I turned the corner and saw the red stone and the spire. I went towards the door, imagining, in fear and hope, that when I entered, the fabric, or my mind, would break.

I stood beside one of the great pillars and waited. I came out after a few minutes, and stood still. 'Sonja,' I said, half loud, 'I will do what good I can.'

CHAPTER XIII

It was about a week later. I was making the round of my phonetics class, from one student to the next, closing my eyes as they repeated the sounds after me and thinking that I might lose my balance in the darkness. When I came to Claire Endrich and met her steady look, I wondered how much she knew.

I came out of the University on to the alley way where Sonja used to wait for me at a discreet distance. The high grey-yellow walls, facing each other across the narrow ascent, held rigidly between them empty space.

At the end of term I went and saw my professor, and said that, having had an unhappy experience, I was thinking of not coming back. After I had told him briefly of Sonja's death, he asked me whether I had a 'Schuldgefühl', a feeling of guilt. I cannot remember whether I answered 'Yes' or 'No'. He was kind and said they would be sorry to lose me, and that I should wait before deciding.

In these first weeks I kept hearing in my mind a phrase from a Bach prelude which suddenly and slowly the organist had begun to play as at the end of the funeral service all rose, Dr Oettinger and his wife on my either hand. I had not heard the music before, but I seemed to know it. I listened with eyes lowered; for in front of me, before the altar, was the coffin, heaped with flowers from other people. Through the music I caught the sound of a metallic click. Looking up quickly, I saw that the flowers and wreaths were jerkily sinking down from sight. Then the music had ceased.

Sometimes I thought I saw her among the crowds, and wondered whether I was acting, as when I had thought in Zürich that I saw myself.

Whether or not I came back to Basle, I could not stay any longer in the same rooms, so I started to pack my books and belongings. I opened the small Virgil, and read again 'Fit Beroë conjunx'; looked through the album she had made, painting the parchment cover with her children's flowers, for our photographs from Lake Constance; and took out from its envelope

149

the illuminated 'I' which I had given her at Strasbourg. My letters to her, neatly bundled and dated, I didn't read.

Sometimes I thought of her making her preparations and in her thoughtfulness for others leaving everything in order, then sitting in the kitchen in the darkness, hearing the hiss of the gas, resisting the instinct to live, until resistance clouded.

I was standing on the kerb where the five main streets of Basle met, and as I waited to cross, I watched the policeman with his baton ordering the traffic. On two of the corners, jutting out like headlands, were the head offices of banks. One of them – the People's Bank – I had just left, having closed the savings account and taken out the money, the equivalent of about thirty pounds. Up the hill a green tram came grinding and stopped, and the policeman signalled to the people to cross. As I remained on the kerb, it came back to me how I had thought after Strasbourg, walking against the midday stream of people, that Sonja and I in the cathedral and in my speaking of marriage had been in a different world from this.

The Burkhardts had read of Sonja's death, and asked me to spend a Sunday with them. It turned out a perfect summer's day, and we all went a walk along the Rhine. After the children had been put to bed and I had gone up to see them, Herr and Frau Burkhardt and I had supper in the garden beneath the cherry tree. Before we went indoors because it was growing cool, we stood on the flagged terrace at the end of the lawn and looked across to the silhouette of Basle, the Münster spire like a single sharp thorn, against the evening sky. Frau Burkhardt stood with her bony wrist upon her husband's sleeve; and when, removing her arm, she turned to go indoors, her dress of blue Egyptian cotton swinging loose and empty upon her gaunt frame, I thought how unaware she was that it was she who was living against forgotten death. We sat and talked a little longer, and Frau Burkhardt told me how only a few weeks ago she had seen me and Sonja walking over the Rhine bridge, arm in arm, 'as if you were going home'. 'This is sentimentality.' I thought, seeing ourselves through her eyes and believing her. As I went away, Herr Burkhardt gripped my hand in sympathy; she kissed me, and I felt her hard rigid body. Walking back in the falling darkness, I thought that that body had borne children, and I remembered imagining on Sonja's face an ex-

150

pression of beatitude if to her gentle breasts she were to hold our child. I remembered how Dr Oettinger had said as we came back from the crematorium that I had given Sonja the experience of love, and that I could not have done more, for she was not the kind of woman to be happy as a wife. I wanted to believe that he was right, and told myself that if with her whole being she had wanted me to marry her, she could and would have made me. But the thought brought no relief. I passed the cornfield where we had walked on the first evening and I had plucked an ear and caressed her cheek; and in the milky summer starlight the standing corn belonged to the world of coming day, where I was alive.

CHAPTER XIV

I was in Germany, on the way to Paul. The train slowly drew up at a platform, and from my corner seat I watched the waiting passengers bunching and jostling. Two jack-booted, brown-shirted Nazis marched past the window, with nothing but the glass between me and them.

I looked round the room at the familiar pictures Paul had bought during the inflation. 'That is new,' I remarked, and picked up from the writing-desk a small Greek figure of a dancing satyr. 'It has a curious freedom', Paul said.

Probably, I thought, he hoped that after Sonja's death I would turn to him. Though he did not say that he and I should work together, he spoke of the urgent need to formulate the principles of a European cultural communism; for the fascists were exploiting and perverting, while the communists denied, the reality of Western culture.

From Highgate I wrote to my professor in Basle and said that I would be coming back.

I learned the Bach prelude which the organist had played in Sonja's memory; and my stepmother, who had grown worse, often made signs to me to play it.

If everything was not to be meaningless, I must go on as I had begun. One day before I left again for Basle, I found my way to King Street and bought the *Daily Worker*.

My room was on the top floor of a six-storey block of flats, with airy views down a broad, busy street and over a small park. The desk, where I sat working at lectures on 'Socialism in English Literature', was at the window giving on the park, and as my eyes followed the people walking quickly across from corner to corner or strolling among the playing children, my brain seemed empty. I repeated to myself Goethe's line, 'Denn alle Schuld rächt sich auf Erde'. God is not mocked. There is deadness in me now because I refused to live. Then I said to myself, 'This is religion', and put Sonja out of my mind.

I began to read Marx's *Capital*, and was pleased when I felt that I had grasped the distinction between the concrete work which creates use-value and the abstract work which creates money-value. As I thought about them, I associated concrete work with the memory of standing beside my father in his workshop and of how I had helped him when he was building the house at Ruislip and my cold, clammy hands had been warm and dry. I disliked, as if with personal dislike, the abstract value through which concrete work became embodied in the commodity and perverted into an object to be bought and sold for money. I had pleasure from Marx's description of the antics performed by a commodity since it was at one and the same time both abstract and concrete, and of its dancing like a Chinese table.

This term Claire Endrich came to my diminished conversation class. She spoke well and was quick-minded and provocative, eager to contradict all the commonplaces of conversation, including mine; when she was arguing with another student against Swiss sympathy with Hitler, she looked towards me, as if confirming an understanding between us. Once the conversation turned to amateur theatricals, and I said that it would be good practice to do an English play. The students liked the idea, and we chose *The Dark Lady of the Sonnets,* Claire to play the Dark Lady. For movement and action we rehearsed in the English Seminar; for pronunciation and expression, the students came singly to my room. Tension began to gather between Claire and me; and one evening, after she had got up to go away, I kissed her. The words came into my head, 'Marry me'.

Soon afterwards, as I was having supper in a restaurant, I knew that I was ill, and for over a week I was in bed with a high temperature. I dreamt continuously, both at night and in the daytime. The dream I never forgot was of pieces of money, covered on their upper face with writhing maggots, that oscillated downwards through translucent green water to the bottom of the sea and its sediment of worms. Never had I discovered in my mind such loathsomeness.

I remembered having once gone with Hans and Elsa to an open-air swimming pool outside Basle, and as we sat on the grass after our bathe, Elsa said, 'Look at that boy over there lying under the tree. He has a mother complex; he's caressing his paps'. I now began to do the same, and noted the indifference that made me capable of forgetting the reality of

153

Sonja's death to give myself the pleasure of playing at being her. Then I thought: 'If I am thinking of myself as a woman, by whom do I imagine myself possessed?' The answer that came was 'A storm-trooper'; and I was afraid at what was happening to me.

Upon the brown patterned carpet, near to my bed, was a patch of sunlight, brightening and shrinking and brightening again. As I watched it moving in and out of itself, I remembered sitting in the loft at Ruhleben after I had heard of Graeme's death, and seeing the sunlight dazzling on the canal; and how at the thought of writing a poem, I had seen him dead at my feet. I had been indifferent also to that death.

As I lay, I let the associations to the pieces of money in the dream come into my head. Thinking of the thirty pieces of silver, I remembered listening to the St John Passion with Sonja in the Münster, and how at Peter's inconsolable crying after his denial of Christ the tears had come into my eyes, and I had asked myself whom I had betrayed. If through its images, I suddenly thought, the dream expressed how that betrayal had corrupted me, then what it was in me that formed the dream must still be true to what I had betrayed. But how to reach that truth? Then the money made me think of the abstract value of the commodity, in which I felt the same indifference as in myself; whereas, helping my father build the house and doing concrete work, then I had felt whole and sound. Perhaps what has gone wrong with me is not because of my own quality, but because, living in this society, I am a commodity. I repeated it to myself, 'I am a commodity'; and it sounded rather a joke.

I dropped off to sleep, and when I woke up daylight was almost gone.

There was a ring, and I heard the landlady go to the door. A woman came in, her face bright beneath her fur cap, for it was cold outside, carrying a large hamper with fruit, a bottle of cognac and a cold chicken which, she said, was from herself and her four friends whose houses I went to in turn one evening in the week so that they could talk English. Usually I had supper first with her and her husband, and then she and I walked to the house where the group was to meet; and the walks were a pleasure to us. One evening in the first beginning

154

of summer we had come to a great chestnut tree in full blossom, and each shared the other's joy. She unpacked the hamper, and told me to eat every bit of the chicken. 'And come back to us,' she said. 'We miss you.'

Claire came, her arms full of flowers which at this wintry time must have cost her far more than she could afford, for her mother was separated from her husband and lived on a small allowance. She got vases from the landlady, and presently the flowers were brightening the room. 'There!' she said, and gave me a quick kiss.

'There's going to be a fight at the University,' she said. 'You must get better quickly.' The Burschenschaft to which the sons of old Basle families belonged had announced a public meeting at which a German professor would give a lecture entitled 'The Philosophy of the People'. 'He's a fascist,' said Claire. 'We want to attack him in the discussion. You must help us. You must, must, must get better. You've got a week.' I said that I thought it would be all right.

The meeting was held in a room above a restaurant, reproductions of paintings by Cézanne hanging on the buff, panelled walls. I sat down on a chair at the end of a row. Nearer to the front I saw Claire sitting between two young men, her head bent as they both talked to her. Most of the audience – there were fifty or sixty people there – looked like students, some of them wearing the Burschenschaft ribbon.

Escorted by two students, the speaker entered, fair-haired, elderly, but vigorous and hale. After a few remarks, the chairman called on him to speak on 'The Philosophy of the People', and I got my pencil ready.

'You are the people,' he began, 'and you are gathered together. That is your philosophy.' When each of us was by himself, he was not himself. We became ourselves when we gathered together. This was the primeval life experience, first within the family, then within the nation, to which all philosophers hitherto, corrupted by bourgeois individualism and Jewish intellectualism, had been blind. The people, not the individual, thinks; and the people's philosophy is the National Socialist Revolution.

As a silence in the discussion lengthened, I found myself on my feet. This meeting, I said, was not a mystic unity. I and

155

others were in disagreement with the speaker. The family was not a mystic unity either, for it was founded on private property, and contained within itself all the contradictions of a society founded on private property. Therefore the nation was not a unity, and philosophy should be the recognition of conflict. I sat down; and in the hostile silence there was a loud clapping from Claire's small group, and she turned and nodded excitedly.

When the meeting was over, I joined Claire and her companions to talk over a drink. One of them I knew by sight, as he came to my lectures on 'Socialism in English Literature'; another was a science student, acquainted with Hans Riemann, and the third a Jewish refugee from Poland. They discussed what to do next, and decided to form a students' anti-fascist committee and to start a journal, to be called *Avantgarde*. They asked me if I would help, and I said that I would.

Claire came to tea next day. She had a bunch of violets at her breast, and she unfastened them and put them in my hand. Then she locked the door.

As we made love, again the words came into my head, 'Marry me'. But I felt that I was saying them to nothingness.

CHAPTER XV

At Christmas I went to meet Paul on the lake of Titisee in the Black Forest.

He said that things were rapidly getting worse in Berlin. Only the previous week, going round to a café to meet some writers and artists, he had found it boarded up, wrecked by storm-troopers. If he found it impossible to stay on in Berlin, I said, he could come to Basle for a year, and we could manage.

Early in the beginning of 1933 Hitler became Chancellor. Late one night in March I was going home across the Markt-platz after giving a lecture on English humour to an Anglo-Swiss Club in a room with large mirrors; there had been a mirror on the wall facing me, so that I had had to see myself lecturing in it, and I was still haunted by my double. There was a crowd outside a newspaper office. Going over, I saw written in bold letters across a big sheet of paper pasted on the glass of the window, 'Der Reichstag brennt!' The Reichstag was in flames; and it was said that the fire had been started by the communists. It was like the eve of the war, when in Halle the groups collected round the placards. I was uncompre-hending: why had the communists done it? Then I thought, 'The Nazis themselves have started it'; and a man's angry voice said from the crowd, 'That's provocation against the com-munists and the Jews'.

Next morning Claire came with the latest editions of the newspapers. 'I told my mother,' she said. 'It was the fascists. My father rang her up and said it was the communists, and she believes him.' There was a report that a communist member of the Reichstag had gone to the police to tell them that he had had nothing to do with the fire. 'He's an odd kind of Marxist,' I said. 'He's supposed to fight the State, not plead to it his innocence.'

The students' anti-fascist group organized a meeting, at which Claire took the chair. As she stood up, I could feel that she was trembling; but she spoke well, and the spirit of the meeting was high.

Paul wrote a few days later to say that he would be coming

157

in a fortnight, and I took a three-roomed flat above a grocer's shop in a pleasant tree-lined street.

A van arrived with Paul's belongings, and the two connecting front rooms were filled with his pictures, the Greek and Roman heads, a painted Gothic wooden Madonna, and his grand piano. My room, with French windows and a railed balcony, looked on to the backs of tall houses, so near that from my desk I could not see the sky.

With private lessons and teaching English at a commercial school, Paul was soon making enough money not only to keep himself but to lead the same kind of life as in Berlin. He became friendly with antique and picture dealers, through whom he met leading artists in Basle. He became acquainted with my professor and invited him to dinner in the flat. He took me to Sunday afternoons given by the professor of psychology, at which he met two women with whom he soon started affairs.

Not long after he had come, he went to bed for some days, saying that he had the flu. After I had brought his supper, he would sit up against his pillows and talk about the book he was going to write on 'the three realities'; and I remembered how I had thought in Camp that he was like a child telling stories to his mother, so that she would not go away. I knew that he would not write the book.

He used to start work early, getting up two or three hours before me, and then come to breakfast in a dark, corded dressing-gown, which, with the balding patch in his light-brown hair, gave him the appearance of a monk.

When Claire came round to the flat and the three of us were having a drink in Paul's room, I felt, as I had when he had met Sonja, that it was I who was the third person. We argued fiercely about the nature of reality. I was reading about Eddington's double table – the table I thought I worked at and the table of empty space and atoms; and I denied this duality. Paul replied that Eddington's table was the expression of Western culture in its third phase of collective science, and that my 'real table' was naïve religious materialism and Philistine indifference to cultural creativeness. When I doggedly repeated 'Reality is reality', Claire said in a disappointed tone, 'Can't you say anything more than that?'

Sometimes, when Claire was making a lunch for us and the

three of us were in the small kitchen, I stood silent, watching Paul flirt with her and thinking how she would say, when she and I were alone, 'Say something nice to me', and I would be dumb, and she would go moody. But he pleased her and made her more alive than I did, because he himself was more alive; and energy is truth. Then I went and stood at the window of my room and looked at the house-backs. 'I am in prison again', I thought.

Most days we played duets together. Once, in the slow movement of a Haydn symphony, I had to come in with a single beautiful phrase, and I played it without thought. 'Alick!' Paul cried. 'Not like that. Feel it.' And he sang it as it should be played. And I played it again, quivering with fury and thinking that because it was Paul who had made me feel its beauty I was ready to kill a phrase of music, and that I was trembling because I wanted to kill him.

In the early summer Claire and I went away for some days to a mountain village where she had been to school as a small child and which she greatly loved; and we were happier. But one morning, on the way to a high Alpine meadow, we were climbing up a mountainside so steep that I went down on hands and knees. Feeling behind me the unseen declivity, I was afraid, as if the mountain-side would heel over and throw me into nothingness. We reached the top and lay down on the short, fine, sweet grass, and Claire dozed off. As I lay with my eyes shut, I felt the earth turning and the fear coming back. Then the feeling passed, and I also slept.

Before we went back to Basle, we agreed that it would be a good idea to get married. Perhaps I was now marrying her, I thought, because I knew I should have married Sonja, but at the same time justifying myself for not having done so because this marriage rejected as reactionary what marriage with Sonja would have been. We spoke of having a deed drawn up by which we would be free to leave each other.

On our return to Basle, Claire and I began studying *Capital*, and I prepared questions for us to discuss each day. I was also reading Marx's articles on India, since I was lecturing on the British Empire, beginning with the early merchant adventurers.

Paul had got stuck in his work, but he was all the more insistent that he was facing the issue which I was evading. He had been reading my lectures on 'Socialism in English Literature'. 'You haven't lectured on socialism in English literature,' he said. 'You have made literature into sociological material and picked out what suits you. You impoverish both literature and socialism because you relate neither to the organism of Western culture.'

'Your cultural organism,' I replied, 'is the Catholic Church from which you have never freed yourself. When you criticize my understanding of socialism, you don't want me to go forward to real socialism; you want me to come back and serve your cultural religion.'

Not long afterwards, I was sitting at my table correcting students' translations of a story by Thomas Mann. Behind the pile of exercise books was the Chinese vase which I had given to Sonja, and there were tall marguerites in it which Claire and I had picked on a walk. As I searched for ways to improve the students' sentences, my eyes stayed on the flowers.

I felt the movement of the white petals holding themselves open round the yellow centre. 'Feel it,' Paul had said when I played without thought the musical phrase. Now I seemed to live in the flower. 'Why shouldn't I?' I thought. If I identify myself with reality, that would be a way out. I kept looking at the flowers: one distinct from the other; and in them all, the common living against silence, like music. 'When I look thus with attention,' I said to myself, 'what I feel is love.' I remembered 'Thou shalt love thy neighbour as thyself.' If I did, I should not feel, if I went on, as I must, instead of back to God and the culture, that I was doing wrong. Paul wanted me to worship an organic unity of culture, different from the real activity of culture as God was different from the world; and because I wanted to worship and had worshipped, I felt evil if I didn't. But if I loved reality, I should be all right.

I got up and went to the window. As I looked at the house-backs which I had called my prison, they became my prison no longer. They were ugly, yet they were unspeakably beautiful; for they seemed to have been built in this moment by men who had gone away, but were still somewhere to be found.

At the end of the summer term, Claire and I went to a meeting, held by the Swiss Communist Party, on Hitler's economic policy. In the audience I recognized a very gentle-faced man

160

who had been coming to my lectures on the British Empire, and at the end of the meeting he came up and spoke to us, and invited us to a drink. He worked on the *Basler Vorwärts*, a communist newspaper, he told us; he had come to my lectures because he was specially interested in Britain, and found the facts that I gave useful and new to him, particularly about the slave trade and the beginnings of the empire. He had good friends in England, he said, looking at me mildly through thick glasses; and he gave me a card of introduction to the assistant editor of the *Labour Monthly,* and asked me to give him his best wishes. I told Claire, as we were walking back to her mother's flat through the old part of Basle, that I had been thinking I ought to join the Communist Party. She agreed.

About a fortnight after coming home to Highgate, I called at the office of the *Labour Monthly* and presented the card of introduction. The assistant editor, H. Rathbone, was friendly and interested in conditions in Switzerland, about which I now found I knew little. I told him that I had a friend who was anxious to meet him (I had told Paul of the introduction, and he was also in England staying with his parents), and we arranged to have dinner together.

My stepmother's brother, in whose flat I had stayed in Cairo, was home on leave, and his company lightened my father's depression. After breakfast, my uncle would say 'H.M.S. Queen Elizabeth', holding out to my father a packet of cigarettes with two protruding like fifteen inch guns, and my father, as he took one, was glad to laugh as if the joke were new. My father and I went for our walks and had tea at Kenwood. We talked a little about Germany and fascism, but neither of us wanted argument. I said nothing about Claire.

I read again Graeme's book, and at his words 'To defy the whole system, to refuse to be an instrument of it – this *I* should have done' I thought that if he had lived he would have joined the Communist Party, and that for him I must do what he would have done. But the decision was still to make. Sitting in the drawing-room after my father and stepmother had gone up to bed, the piano still open on which I had played for her the Bach prelude, I felt as if I were being watched.

It had been raining, and then the sun had come out, and we were having tea on the flagged terrace. You could see right across north-east London to the hazy distance of Essex, and two or three miles away the wet roofs of the houses in the sunlight were a pattern of shining rectangles on a blue ground. It was like a cubist picture, and as I wondered at it, I thought that in this picture there were people, and imagined how, looking towards us, they would see, as I had seen looking up Gower Street, after I had watched the demonstration crossing it with red banners, the brow of Highgate heights and the hazy spire of St Michael's. And at one pinprick in their picture, the reality which they didn't know was my father, stepmother and I, sitting here together. The meaning of 'I' changed: the people invisible for me in my pattern of bright rectangles were also living their lives; they also were all 'I' and 'I' and 'I', among the shining roofs of extending London.

I went back to the office of the *Labour Monthly,* and told Rathbone that I would like to join the Communist Party. He said that, as I was not living in England, he would have to make enquiries and would let me know. I asked if there was anything I could do in the weeks before I went back to Switzerland; and he asked me if I would like to have some experience on the *Daily Worker.* I answered that I would; I was having the *Basler Vorwärts* sent to me, so perhaps I could cut out and translate news about Germany. Rathbone said we would talk more about it when he met Paul and me for dinner in a few days time.

It was a friendly evening, Paul talking knowledgeably about Berlin. Before we separated, Rathbone said that I could go to the *Daily Worker* in Tabernacle Street any afternoon, and Paul also, if he wished.

We found the premises in a drab side-street, and went up a dark flight of stairs into a big loft with bare boards, crowded with small tables, and men sitting at them and moving quickly between them and standing in intent conversation amidst the rattle of typewriters. Always when I came to the head of the stairs – I went about ten times before returning to Switzerland – I felt on the brink of an absorbed urgency of people working with a pressure which this old building could hardly support.

On the first day we got curious looks. Page Arnot welcomed us and helped me. Next day's *Daily Worker* contained a paragraph for which I had provided a heading and a report taken from the *Basler Vorwärts* of how on the walls of a town hall the German workers had painted 'Befreit Thälmann'.

For a year or more I had been reading the *Daily Worker*, feeling it a violator of the ideal region of the printed word where the *Morning Post* recorded the news of yesterday. These men, each with his own responsibility, all had their energy bent on the paper for tomorrow and on the revolutionary future. Once the pen jerked uncontrollably in my hand. Perhaps my body would break me. I looked across at Paul: at a nearby trestle-table he was writing away as if at his own work. As I wrote the next sentence, about wheat prices, letter by letter, with my pen in a cramped grip, I heard an angry voice from the other side of the room: 'Never say Russia. Always say the Soviet Union.'

The words came back as I walked up Highgate Hill. You mustn't say 'Russia' because there is no longer the Russia whose fleet, when I was ten years old, had passed our coasts in the night on its way to war – 'Whose side are you on?' we had asked, and I had said 'Japan' – and whose emperor Stephen Dedalus had called 'a sodden Christ'. To say 'Russia' was to revive that empire. The name must be excised because the power in that shape upon the map is not old and national, but new and revolutionary, the same power as in the making of the *Daily Worker;* and it must be called by its name.

I went to a meeting at the Kingsway Hall called by the committee which had been set up to demand the release of Dimitrov, whose trial was soon to begin at Leipzig. The hall was packed to the roof. I had been at theatres and concerts in the Albert Hall; now for the first time I was one of a body of people who wanted not only to see and hear but to do. The excitement and unity mounted, and there was a storm of applause when Harry Pollitt got up from his seat on the platform and stepped forward, and in dead silence began .

Never had I seen such a man, nor heard such oratory. Drawn towards him, the whole hall, tier upon tier of people, became a great wave curving over to break, as his impetuous, unconquerable voice soared and struck and rang, 'Fight fascism'.

When I had got back to Basle, Claire and I decided that we would marry in the spring. Then when she got her degree, we would leave and move to England, for I realized that I wanted to join the Communist Party in my own country.

Paul came with Claire's family to the station to see us off to Lugano for our honeymoon, as we had to call it. He sold his piano and some of his paintings, and went to the Soviet Union until the autumn of that year, 1934. On our return to England, we still met from time to time.

I gave notice at the University, and while Claire worked for her examination I prepared my last course of lectures, on the English newspaper from its beginnings to the present day.

We were now in touch with the Communist Party in Basle and were asked to lead a discussion group, to which six or ten workers came for some weeks, on the Soviet and bourgeois film; and I wrote a poem in German – Save Thälmann! – for mass declamation, rehearsed it with a group of men and girls, and when I heard it in a small crowded hall I was moved that what I had written should be given power by the united voices. I also did dramatic criticism for the *Basler Vorwärts,* occupying the seat allocated to the paper's representative in the stalls of the Stadttheater.

Claire and I were also asked if we could give meals and accommodation in our flat to workers from Germany. They were in Switzerland illegally, and if they were picked up by the Swiss police they were put across the French frontier; sometimes they were back again within an hour, the risk hanging over them that if they were picked up a second and a third time they might be put over the German frontier.

Throughout the summer Klaus came to us often for meals and occasionally stayed the night – why, we didn't ask. He was a few years older than Claire, short and swarthy. After lunch, we sometimes went bathing in the Rhine. Klaus would swim like an otter; and then, the wet drops glistening on his tawny body, he walked on the grass on his hands, and went off to sleep in the full sun. He woke up, and we had a drink from the thermos, and he taught us German revolutionary songs. He was silent about what he had done in Germany, except that once he told us how he and a comrade had climbed a factory chimney at night and on its top fastened the red flag. Of Hitler and fascism he spoke with confident contempt. He wondered that we should have so many books, handled them with respect, and took all the German translations I had of Soviet novels,

164

and books on Dürer and Breughel. He did sketches of Claire and caricatures of me, with a slight roll of fat at the back of my neck, and lino-cuts – in a deserted street at night two men, while a third kept watch, painted on a wall 'Nieder mit Hitler'. He asked for our criticism; and when he had gone back to his room, wherever that might be, we would discuss what it would be best to say; he had not much talent, and we, having no knowledge, felt our inadequacy. Always in his presence I was aware of my comfortable security – still a lecturer at the University, married and in a three-roomed flat, with the freedom and the means to buy railway tickets any day and to travel with my passport in a safe world to England, where I had two thousand pounds capital. In this knowledge, I existed in unseen separation from him, who knew that nothing in coming time was certain for himself, not even until this night, but believed that the future of mankind was his because communism will triumph.

In the autumn, Heinrich came to us. He had already been picked up by the Swiss police. He was only a little younger than I, colourless, with thinning hair, like a schoomaster who cannot keep order. Once when we were sitting in the front room looking out on the street, he saw two men coming towards the house, and jumped up quickly. 'Detectives!' he said. I took him to the balcony at the back where there was a jumble of packing-cases left from Paul's removal, and told him to hide if he heard the men come; but he had been alarmed needlessly. After he had been coming to us for two or three months, he said that he had had instructions to leave Basle, so I gave him a suit, hoping that in my respectable blue serge he would feel, and be, safer. When he had put it on, he smiled at himself in the glass and then at us.

Having packed up for removal to England, we moved into a furnished room and Claire received her degree. Coming back from a week-end in the mountains, we were told by the landlady that in our absence detectives had been; but as we were very soon leaving for England, she let us stay on. Perhaps, I thought, we might have been expelled from the country if it had not been for Dr Oettinger, whom I imagined telling the authorities that Herr West was not dangerous.

We arrived in England early in 1935.

CHAPTER XVI

Joining the Communist Party was my own free act. Having joined it, I belonged to an organization, and my activity as member was not determined by me alone. The Party decided the policy to be pursued, and on me was the obligation to do my part in carrying it out.

I felt that obligation not as the loss but as the gaining of freedom. I had lived as member of the bourgeois class without knowing it; now my life was conscious. The policy which I must put into practice was based upon Marxism, and I believed that I had come to understand Marxism and that in my own person I could contribute to the life of the Party. I was asked to take a course at Marx House with D. M. Garman, who in the twenties had edited *The Calendar of Modern Letters*, on 'Marxism and Literature'; and I was glad and spoke with assurance.

I felt this to be the continuation of the same intellectual activity as when I had studied *Capital* at Basle, but whereas I had been then alone in my mind, maintaining against Paul what I believed to be true, I now took part in common discussion. Garman and I planned together the course on literature and Marxism, and we asked the class to criticise our lectures and to make proposals how the course could be improved. I attended meetings of the Writers Group of the Party, whose purpose was to clarify what we must do as writers for the victory of the Party and of the revolution.

We spoke with each other in the knowledge that we were all members of the Party. And we knew that what made our membership real was not only our belief in Marxism and our adherence to Party policy, nor the holding of a Party card and the paying of dues; we were still members only in name unless we were active in our local Branch. Activity in a basic unit of the Party was necessary to our work as writers. It was for us to express in literary form the essential truth, as embodied in Marxism, of the world in which we lived. Society was in movement, and the energy of that movement was in the conflict between capitalism and socialism. It was our responsibility to heighten men's consciousness of the freedom and abundance of life which through the socialist revolution it was now in their power to win. But we could not heighten that consciousness in others unless we ourselves were inspired by it; and the revolution would remain for us, as intellectuals, an idealist abstraction unless we took part in the activity necessary to its achievement. This activity was the organized fight of the working class to which through its policy the Party gave leadership, to be made effective all over the country through the local branches. In our work in our local branch we were part of the revolutionary movement, and without that active participation we could not think or write as Marxists, since Marxism is the unity of theory and practice.

Claire and I belonged to the Brixton branch, having chosen this part of London because Palme Dutt had advised us not to go and live where the Party membership was likely to be as middle-class as we were.

A young Scottish engineer came to fetch us to our first meeting, and in a small third-floor back room we were introduced as 'New comrades from Switzerland' to the other members: a building worker, an electrical technician, a bank clerk, an unemployed engineer, a school teacher, and a housewife. The meeting began. A letter was read out from the Party centre on the growing menace of fascism and the necessity for the speediest mobilization of the working class of London, and the secretary reported on the local activity of the Blackshirts, who held regular meetings in Brockwell Park and had pitches where they sold their paper, *Action*. It was decided to go out chalking in the streets, and Claire and I said we would come. Five of us went out late one night and across several side-streets where they ran into Brixton Road chalked 'Fascism means Hunger and War'. I stood at a corner to keep a look-out for the police, while the stooped figures chalking the roadway jerkily advanced sideways. I was tense, for we were breaking the law.

We joined up with other Branches of the Party to go on poster parades through Brixton, Clapham and Tooting on crowded Saturday afternoons. On my poster I carried one word of our slogan against fascism and war. I walked close to the kerb, on my left hand the throng of people on the pavement

167

and on my right the buses and cars overtaking us with a safe clearance. We went steadily on. 'Why am I happy,' I wondered, 'and why do I feel that I have never seen a street before? When as my usual self I walk along a street, I never look. Now I am aware that the street is living with people, going where they want to go, that in the roadway are two opposing rivers, and that the road itself bears to right or left and runs straight on as it was first trodden by people's feet. The street lives, and we are its unregarded voice.' Then I thought that I was happy not only because I was doing what I knew to be right, but because, following at regulation distance the comrade ahead of me, I was freed from responsibility.

We met outside The Horns at Kennington to march to Trafalgar Square. By this time we were at our ease with the other members of the Branch and they with us; and when we turned up at the rallying-point, Jim Summers, the building worker, would say with gibing friendliness, 'Here come our intellecticles'. Our red banner was raised – Brixton Communist Party – and far ahead of us also rose the red banners. Singing the International, we entered the Square, while beside us walked the impassive police.

Since we had few speakers in the Branch, I volunteered to do a meeting at our pitch opposite Lambeth Town Hall. I was to speak on colonial independence. I prepared a twenty minute speech with the theme that a nation that oppresses others cannot itself be free, and that our brutal rule in the colonies was our form of fascism. I had learned the speech by heart, and after the chairman's introductory remarks I mounted the rickety red platform, which shook with my trembling. The small audience, with an elderly couple and their dispirited dog standing on the kerb some yards off, were unmoved. But nobody went away, and there was a little clapping as I got down. Jim slapped me on the shoulder: 'Fine,' he said. After the meeting we went and had a drink, and as we were standing at the bar he said again that I had spoken well. Then to my surprise he said, 'But you're too subjective'.

His judgment stuck in my mind because it confirmed my own misgivings. When I was marching with Claire on demonstrations, I had sometimes felt that the purpose of the demonstration and its effectiveness in achieving that purpose mattered less to me than my sense of moral and emotional fulfilment in being part of it. About a year after we had returned to England, standing with Claire on the edge of a great crowd in Hyde Park, I could see George Allison on the high platform, dramatically silhouetted against a rainy sunset sky, his right arm raised, as his urgent voice cried vehemently, 'The time is ripe and rotten ripe for revolution!' 'All to the Albert Hall!' called the chairman as he closed the meeting, for that same evening there was to be a mass rally of Mosley's Blackshirts. We raced across the Park, and the pavement outside the Albert Hall was already packed with a moving throng, and the shouts of 'Down with Mosley!' were like a roaring conflagration. Men and women boarded the buses that were halted in the roadway, and leaning far out of the top windows they shouted into the lamp-lit din 'Fascism means war!' As I stood on the kerb, shouting our slogans with all the power of my lungs, one of four mounted policemen blocking an entrance to the Hall suddenly whipped his horse round so that I had to jump back from its rump, and I was filled with momentary fury. Now, I thought, I know in my body what Lenin meant when he spoke of the special bodies of armed men who uphold by force the power of the state which the revolution is to smash. But when the commotion was left behind and we came up from our underground station into the familiar uneventful street, I felt that in my body I didn't believe that the time was ripe for revolution, and that I gave no thought to the question how and when we should smash the state.

I remembered Paul saying to me 'You are a born compromiser'; and I was still not whole-hearted. I was once selling the *Daily Worker* outside Stockwell underground station. The newsvendor selling the evening papers on the other side of the entrance hadn't objected to my interloping. He shouted with full voice and open throat 'StarnewsanStandard', and I occasionally called out, hardly louder than my speaking voice, 'Buy the *Daily Worker*'. Many of the people passing in and out didn't see me; some gave me an expressionless glance; a few eyed the paper I was holding up and the *Daily Worker* poster tied round my waist. I stood there, the life going on around me. I am a support for a poster, I thought, a stand for a newspaper, and behind this show for others I can safely go

169

on being myself. I thus dissociate what I feel to be 'I' from my appearance as Party member. As Ananias withheld his money, so I withhold myself. 'I' is for me a bourgeois concept, a secret escape from Communist being. Yet in this recognition I also want to make myself a communist.

Being thus concerned with what happened inside my head, and afraid to lose the emotional assurance gained through Party membership, I was not free to face my doubts whether the Party itself was in the right.

One Saturday in the summer of 1936 I was selling the *Daily Worker* with Jim Summers outside Norwood bus garage. It contained a statement that in our fight against fascism we must defend bourgeois democracy and national sovereignty. 'What's got into them?' Jim asked. 'Do they want us to wave the Union Jack?' I replied that those who would not fight fascism to win socialism would fight it because they believed in their own country, and so we could build unity. But I convinced neither him nor myself.

Such unity, I thought, was not unity, but a tactical and temporary agreement. It was not a question of building unity, but of arousing the power of the unity in which we necessarily lived as members of society, and which our theory of fascism implicitly denied. We said that fascism was the terrorist dictatorship of monopoly capitalism, and this I did not question; but we ignored the fascist movement through which that dictatorship was exercised. Its ideology was more than demagogy subsidized by Krupp; it was a perversion of the truth, which had inspired romanticism, that the individual is part of the universal process of nature and society. 'The bourgeois revolution,' said one of its spokesmen whom I had read when I was in Basle, 'was the revolution of "I"; the national socialist revolution is the revolution of "we".' The fascist movement was able to win the adherence of millions, not only from the petty bourgeoisie, but also from the working class, because through its propaganda of a Germanic culture and through its mass organizations it offered them liberation from the atomized society of capitalism and the prospect of participation in the making of a new order. If we merely dismissed this movement as demagogy, we denied the reality of social being to which fascism appealed.

170

Why, I asked myself, am I thinking thus? This is not Marxism but religion. When I want the Party to recognize our real, existing unity, I am thinking of 'the unknown God, in whom we live and move and have our being'. I am thinking of Paul and his 'three realities', and the cathedral as the expression of the unity of the organic group. In fascist ideology I recognize my own emotion, and under its influence I am saying in effect that there is more truth in fascism than in communism.

So I remained silent. In my activity as member of my Branch I repeated at meetings what I had said to Jim Summers. I remained silent even to myself; and this suppression affected my intellectual work and my relation to the Party.

Besides lecturing at Marx House, I was at this time working on a book, *Crisis and Criticism*, published in 1937. The crisis referred to in the title I described as emotional and intellectual uncertainty centred round 'I' and 'we'. Contemporary criticism and aesthetic theory, as represented by T. S. Eliot and Herbert Read, regarded poetic creation as the activity, not of what people formerly meant by 'I', but of what transcended 'I'. But although 'I' was being abandoned as a category of criticism, there was also a distrust of 'we', which I illustrated with Dr I. A. Richards' quotation, in *Practical Criticism*, from a reader's remark on D. H. Lawrence's poem *Piano*, which describes a man being overcome, as he nears the piano being played, by memories of childhood. The reader said:

> Although I feel almost ashamed to say so this poem makes the biggest appeal . . . The poem seems to me so eminently sentimental (I see no reason why I, a grown man, should allow myself the luxury of tears).

Dr Richards commented:

> A widespread general inhibition of all the simpler expansive developments of emotion (not only of its expression) has to be recognized among our educated population.

I contrasted this uncertainty about 'I' and 'we' with Coleridge's definition of life as 'the *principle of Individuation,* or the power which unites a given *all* into a *whole* that is presupposed

171

by all the parts', and with his conception of the imagination as the power through whose working the unity of poetry and of the body politic, as he termed it, are one. Criticism, I said, must return to this truth that the unity of poetry, in which consists beauty, and the unity of the body politic are the same unity. Marxism has freed this truth from its idealistic form, and we are now conscious that the energy of the body politic is not, as Coleridge said, in God, but in ourselves. The beauty of literature consists in the writer's power imaginatively to become one with the creative activity by which men through their productive labour make nature human and so realize their own humanity; and the perception of beauty by the reader arises from the resultant heightening of his sense of his reality as a human being, a member of society changing the world and itself. To express and to feel this energy of social change, writer and reader must take active and conscious part in bringing the change about, which meant identifying themselves with the working class and the fight for the socialist revolution.

When my father read the book, he said that it had no centre. I think he was right, inasmuch as I had not penetrated to what was for me at the heart of the conflict. For I only described an imaginary bourgeois intellectual torn between socialism and an ideology prior to fascism. When I spoke of the uneasiness about 'I' and 'we', I said nothing about the fascist 'we' nor about its power to release collective emotion. This was the real intellectual and political issue, and the book was weakened because it did not face it.

Because of my uneasiness about unity I felt separated from the Party, though I took part in all the activity of the Branch, directed now to support for Spain – selling pamphlets and special issues of the *Daily Worker;* collecting money for medical supplies; poster parades and demonstrations, and outdoor meetings at which I spoke in Lambeth and elsewhere. We had letters from Klaus and Heinrich, the comrades we had known in Basle, telling us that they had joined the Thaelmann Battalion of the International Brigade.

Flanked by police, Mosley marched his men down into Trafalgar Square. With the comrades from our Branch we stood on the kerb opposite St Martin-in-the-Fields, and the air was filled with the fierce shouting:

172

'Remember Guernica! Arms for Spain! Remember Guernica!'

At the meetings for unity the darkness of the Empress Hall was riven with beams of light, and the fighters of the International Brigade marched into the arena with the Union Jack of the British Battalion. We rose to our feet and the flag was lowered in honour of the fallen heroes: Ralph Fox, Christopher Caudwell, David Guest.

Yet in my mind there remained uneasiness. We reassure those who believe only in bourgeois democracy that the government of the Spanish Republic is not communist. But the movement we ask them to support is directed to a different democracy than theirs. 'We Communists,' the *Manifesto* said, 'scorn to conceal our aims.' We conceal ours for the sake of unity, and all we achieve is a false unity with Gollancz and the Left Book Club; and by that compromise we take away from our own aim its power to inspire real unity.

During 1937 and 1938 I spent a good deal of time in the organizing and running of the Writers and Readers Group of the Left Book Club, which was to bring writers and readers into contact with one another and overcome the separation between writers and readers by uniting them in the fight against fascism, so that literature would be enriched by a new content of political struggle and the content of our political aims would be given definition through artistic form. But when I spoke at meetings on Koestler's *Spanish Testament,* I kept silent about the essence of the book: that when Franco's forces were advancing on Malaga, Koestler, against all political reason and duty, under 'a strange and uncomfortable fascination', as he put it, got out of the car that was taking him from Malaga into Republican territory and was next day arrested by the fascists. Why did he go back unless on him, as on me, fascism exerted an attraction? If we were to defeat fascism, I should force discussion on the source of the attraction.

The sense of separation from the Party was intensified on the outbreak of war.

On the Saturday before war was declared I went down to Victoria Station to meet Heinrich. What happened to Klaus, we never heard; but after the defeat of Spain, Heinrich with hundreds of others of the International Brigade was interned in the south of France. He had written to us and we had got

173

permission for him to come to England and stay with us, and I had had a wire that morning that he was coming. The station was full of parties of small school children being evacuated, 'little objects' as my father would have called them, their gas-masks in the cardboard boxes bobbing behind them as they ran and crowded and hopped up and down around their teacher. Claire also would be gone when I got back, for she had become a teacher and her school was being moved to Brighton.

Heinrich was not on the train. Among the last passengers to come through the barrier was Violet, a member of the committee of the Writers and Readers Group, who had cut short her holiday in France. 'But it's all right,' she said with innocent knowingness. 'Chamberlain will do another Munich.'

That night there was already black-out. I had supper out, and then went to a pub and had two pints of beer. Feeling rather heavy, for I rarely drank more than half a pint, I took the blue-lit tram and barely recognized my stop at the top of Brixton Hill. I remained standing at the kerb, looking at the strange darkness. The cars with screened and hooded headlamps drove slowly, and two policemen by the dimmed traffic lights kept calling to them, 'Your lights are far too bright, Your lights are far too bright.' A wireless was playing in a ground floor flat nearby, and I recognized a Haydn symphony which, arranged for four hands on the piano, I had often played with Paul and then with Sonja. I moved nearer to the partly open window to listen. It was raining hard, and over the brow of Brixton Hill lightning flickered on the clouds. 'War,' I thought. 'This is the end of our world.' Conscious that I was not completely sober, I listened to the music I loved go jubilant to its close, and I was shaken with a loud sobbing I didn't try to control.

Next night, the Sunday that Chamberlain said we were at war, I went down to answer a late ring at the door, and Heinrich was there. We sat in the kitchen, where I had rigged up the black-out, and he ate hungrily what food there was. We talked and he told me that his wife had died in a concentration camp in Germany; yet my memory is that he, a fighter from the International Brigade, and I, a Communist Party member, had no words. Speaking of the Nazi-Soviet pact, he said: 'I don't understand the Soviet Union any longer'. Does even he now speak his doubt, I thought.

174

The sirens had wailed that morning, but there was no sense that we, Britain, were at war, at last fighting fascism. Words from Chamberlain spoken over the air could not suddenly make a national unity. *Who* was fighting fascism? An official Britain that had denied arms to Spain? A Labour Party that had expelled Cripps on the day Barcelona fell? The now collapsed sentimentality of the Left Book Club?

The *Daily Worker* had published the Executive Committee's statement on the war: it was a war against fascism, and therefore the working class must support it; but Chamberlain and the Tories could not be trusted to fight fascism, and therefore while supporting the war the Party must lead the fight for a Labour Government. The Party statement seemed to me another voice on the air. To say that the war was against fascism was to deceive ourselves. The war was being fought by the state, not by us; and the state, being the imperialist state, was not opposed to fascism.

Some weeks later the Executive Committee said that the war was an imperialist war, and the workers must end it 'after their own fashion' – which meant by revolution. That, I thought, makes sense; and with the outbreak of the Finnish war a first duty became clear: to stand up for the Soviet Union, and to tell the truth about Mannerheim, and his crushing of the Finnish Socialist Republic and his slaughter, with German help, of the Finnish workers after the first world war; and to say, as I said at meetings of the Secularist Society which in the last year had been asking me to speak, that he built his Mannerheim Line against the Soviet Union, not to defend freedom but to attack it; and that Chamberlain's deepest desire was to join him and switch the war, and that those who joined in the beery blaring of *We're going to hang out the washing on the Siegfried Line* were deluded. Even after Dunkirk our duty still remained to end the war in our own fashion; and that meant to hold on to class consciousness and not to be tricked into the defence of British imperialism because the English countryside, seen under the threat of invasion, was beautiful and dear. When the air-raids started and the people pushed through the police to go down into the tubes for shelter, we said that this was the beginning of the action by which the people would end the war. In 1941 the People's Convention –

reported and photographed in a special article in *Picture Post*, met in London and demanded peace.

But I took no part in this campaign. Having been employed for a couple of years as English teacher in a Swiss mercantile school and then as a copywriter in an advertising agency until shortly before the outbreak of war, I was now teaching English at the Soviet Embassy, and had been told not to do any open Party work. So when Claire came home late from meetings to organize support for the People's Convention, I would be busy preparing my lessons for the next day or reading a detective story, reluctant to be disturbed; and we began to be estranged.

I had no strong sense of belonging either to the Party or to the nation at war. Nor was I at first affected by the attack on the Soviet Union. When at a great rally behind the British Museum Harry Pollitt called with all the power of his eloquence for the most vigorous prosecution of the war, I thought, as I stood beside one of the stone lions, Claire near me, that Hitler's invasion of the Soviet Union had not changed the relation of class forces in Britain. If now we could say 'We will make this war *our* war and fight with all our might', why could we not have said it and done it before? The resolution 'Everything for the war' was put, and the air quivered with the lifted hands. 'Against?' Stillness. Claire said to me afterwards, 'You didn't do any good by abstaining.'

In the summer of 1942 our marriage came to an end, and I took a furnished room in Kensington Church Street. At the time of Stalingrad, my mood changed. When the evening papers were brought to the attaché or secretary to whom I was giving a lesson, and he would snatch at one and read 'Germans Gain 75 Yards', and grunt and throw it aside and go on with the lesson, I wished I could give more than silence. In the winter I became an air-raid warden. When there was an alarm, I usually went from the post to a shelter at the top of Campden Hill, and having gone in and talked to the people on the wooden benches in the dim light and dank air, I posted myself outside. The ground being high and no houses immediately in front, there was a wide vault of sky over a darkened London; and on the occasional nights of heavy raids I watched the searchlights, the flares floating down, and the bursting stars of the A.A. guns; and beyond all the clamour, the sky. Some-

176

times, in the winter months, when I signed off and went home for breakfast before going to teach at the Soviet Embassy, day was breaking, here and there a light shining uncurtained, danger being over.

I remember returning one morning when the sky was flushed with dawn, and thinking that I was happy. I remember with pleasure many dawns – in the wide sky over the Ruhleben race-course, where our grey ranks stood lined up in the snow for the roll-call; across the empty desert at Lahun; as I walked up Highgate Hill after travelling by night from Dublin and re-solved to keep my mind delighted with the consciousness of the day. On this morning there was a happiness of a different quality because I felt that the now waking streets had been in my keeping in the night.

Leaning far out of the window, I could just make out in the clear morning sky the planes passing over, wave after wave, clear and translucent against the blue, like small fishes, moving slowly. 'Open the Second Front in 1942' we had demanded at our Congress. 'Open the Second Front in 1943.' 'Open the Second Front Now.' This was the beginning, the war coming to its end.

For a time there was exultation. Paris was liberated, not by armies, but by the people with arms. This was the beginning of the new world at peace.

The French communists handed in their arms. Spitfires machine-gunned Athens and the Greek resistance fighters. 'Freedom is not a drab,' said Churchill, 'to be picked up in the streets.' 'Neither is she a rich man's kept mistress,' retorted Compton Mackenzie at a meeting in Trafalgar Square. 'Every-body who was at that meeting ought to be hanged,' a woman warden said to me at the Post. 'I was one of them,' I answered.

Doubt grew almost to certainty that it was not going to be a new world.

In February, 1945, our Kensington Branch was holding a meeting in a church hall to celebrate Red Army Day. In the black-out I saw two or three comrades standing near the entrance to what I supposed to be a passage leading to the hall; I thought, however, that I would not speak to them, but would go in by myself; and as I could see a gleam of light shining from under the door, without flicking on my torch I started down the passage. Next instant I was charging headlong down in blackness. For it was not a passage, but a flight of steps, and the light had not come from under the door but from the transom above. I thought, 'I am plunging into hell'. Though it was a flight of sixteen steps, I remained on my feet, cannoned into the wall at the bottom, and slumped down in the corner. The door opened, and two figures looked at me, motionless. 'You might help me up,' I said plaintively. My right arm was broken, and an ambulance was sent for, and I was taken to hospital.

I was not fully in my right senses, for when my particulars were being taken, including my religion, I protested with unusual violence that I was not C. of E. but an atheist; and when I had been undressed and was being examined by a doctor, I said to him in German: 'I can tell by your accent. You are a refugee from fascism.'

That night, or the next day, I had a dream. Like the dream when I was ill after Sonja's death, it had upon me the effect of a terrible revelation. Within me there was corruption; and again there were crawling worms on the deep bed of the sea.

Sometime on that first day, I opened my eyes and on the table beside the bed was a small green vase with four yellow opening crocuses. Standing at the end of the bed, gravely looking at me, was my sister, Constance.

At first, when I had recovered from shock, and took in my surroundings, I thought I could not stand it. I lay on my back with my right arm outstretched on a wooden support and weights attached, since the arm was broken just beneath the shoulder and because of war conditions no suitable splint was available. A bare, cold green wall with a large white clock faced me, and beneath it a long rigid line of parallel iron beds, whose occupants seemed to guard their own jealous world. But before many days had passed, in the ward I began to feel a collective unsentimental power, and was glad I was not alone. From the patients near me, and from the untiring nurses, came sympathy, but no pity: there are others besides you. In each of us, waking, sleeping, the process of nature in our human body was at work, unceasing day and night. I had to help the others by not being sorry for myself; for not such a self, but a greater power, in me and in them, had to be left free to make us well.

178

In the hours before dawn, when there was stillness in the long, dimly lit ward, the rounded forms beneath the bedclothes looked like the waves of an unmoving sea. By the door the night sister wrote at her table, her face faintly illuminated by the circle of brightness upon her papers. The words from a letter my father had written to me came into my head: 'Say to yourself, dear boy, This also will pass'. One night there was a distant boom from a German V-2 rocket, but the silence absorbed it.

I dreamed that my extended right arm was the bridge across the Rhine at Remagen, and the pain was the weight of the British tanks crossing into Germany. A man came round with the papers every morning, and comrades from the Branch brought me the *Daily Worker* and Party literature. But I didn't encourage them to come. The matron on her rounds with folded arms, like a walking Queen Victoria, stopped at the foot of my bed and inclined her head, and said, 'He is the ideal patient'.

After seven weeks my arm was taken off the extension and put into a sling, so I could sit up, and soon get up. I went round with the early morning tea-trolley, which helped me to walk, and washed up the cups in the scullery. I belonged now with those who would soon be out, but the hospital still ordered time for me. I went and sat on a balcony in the sun, and read *War and Peace*, which my students at the Embassy had brought me, inscribed 'For our dear good teacher'. There was still to-day and tomorrow and the next day and perhaps the day after before I must go back to my own room.

Constance took me in a taxi up Church Street. For the first time after two months I saw the movement and life of people in the streets; houses and gardens; and the chestnut trees of black February were in the green leaf of April sunshine.

I could still walk only with slow steps and my arm was painful if anybody touched it, so I thought I would stay away from the victory celebrations; but in the afternoon I went into Kensington Gardens and sat on the grass near the Round Pond. Out of the blue sky no more bombs would fall. Children were playing near me, and on a gentle slope lovers lay embraced; and this living of human beings in the sunlight, as if there had been no war, seemed more real than war.

179

First from Ruhleben, then from the sanatorium at Arosa, and now from the hospital – this is my third return. What am I going to do this time? I lie alone, without impulse or expectation. I am a Party member, and we have won the war against fascism; yet the future is an emptiness. Tall trees rose on the other side of the Round Pond, where the ground dipped, and I remembered looking at the line of trees after leaving Dr Schmid and thinking for the first time that trees are rooted in the earth. Suddenly they became menacing, a monstrous army advancing over the brow of the slope, and for a few moments I was seized with panic. 'That is how a madman sees the world,' I thought, 'but I am not mad.'

A girl from the Party Branch, with whom I had gone out selling the *Daily Worker,* came to see me. As she lay on the divan, with her legs drawn up and her head propped on her hand, looking at me, I knew that she wanted me to kiss her, but I had no desire, and soon she went away.

I remembered the dream in hospital and the dream in Basle of the money sinking down through the water, and I thought I would write about myself. I filled a couple of pages of an exercise book with a description of a swimmer, his chin on the bright water, and the sunlight patterning his limbs above the sea's sunless depths. Then there was no more impulse to continue writing.

That having failed, I thought more and more of suicide. On the evening before I was to begin teaching again at the Embassy, I stuffed the cracks round the door and between the window-sashes with newspaper, and sat down in the leather armchair beside the fire and turned on the gas; and as I heard the hissing, I thought of Sonja. After not more than a couple of minutes, I got up and turned off the tap, and put the strips of newspaper in the waste-paper basket.

I had used up, I thought, the impulse to suicide when I plunged down the steps. For I had deliberately chosen to go towards the hall alone without speaking to the comrades on the pavement and without turning on my torch; and there must have been in my mind an image of the steps, for I passed the spot almost every day.

Next Morning I went back to work at the Embassy.

180

CHAPTER XVII

The depression lifted, and I felt myself again a member of the Party. At the week-ends I took classes in dialectical and historical materialism, for which I worked at philosophy, particularly Hegel, more than I had yet done. Together with Douglas Garman and Maurice Dobb, I was tutor at a week school held at Netherwood, near Hastings, on the relation between the bourgeois and the socialist revolutions. The syllabus stressed that the bourgeois revolution was not a single act, and that from the beginning, already in the England of the 17th century, it had not been made by the bourgeoisie alone but also by the people, fighting for a freedom beyond bourgeois freedom; in each succeeding phase of the revolution – the French revolution, the revolutions of 1848 – the power of the people increased as the working class arose, organized itself, attained class consciousness, learned from its defeats, until in Russia in 1917 it carried forward the bourgeois revolution into the socialist revolution. So now today the unity which had won victory over fascism in the war must be carried forward by the working class into the victory of socialism.

I was very glad to be asked to do this work. I believed that I was a good tutor; I had once overheard a young worker say to his friend, 'I'd come half across London to have a class with Alick West'. At the week school at Hastings on the bourgeois and socialist revolutions with each day there was, among all those taking part, a growing sense of intellectual exhilaration as we understood more deeply the content and greatness of our purpose, and a comradeship in which we felt the promise of the coming world. On the last evening the students improvised a stage on which they enacted a parody of the school, and I watched with delight the friendly caricature of myself.

Caudwell's *Illusion and Reality* had been republished not long after the war, and I was asked to give the opening address at a conference, with George Thomson in the chair, on the importance of his work. Early in 1936 he had come to the course which Garman and I were taking on Marxism and literature. We knew him then as Christopher Sprigge, and he said nothing about his own writing, though he must already almost have completed *Illusion and Reality* for in November of that year he went to Spain and joined the International Brigade; but at one of the general discussions on the method of the class he said that he thought we were making a mistake in considering the social character of literature without having first considered language. After the class we used to continue the discussion in a pub on Clerkenwell Green, and I have a memory of him standing close to me and considering me with clear eyes, through which I seemed to look into a lucid mind of resolute intelligence.

Caudwell had heightened our understanding, I said at the conference, both of poetry and of our political aim. He started from the assertion that poetry is an economic activity. This was an accepted view inasmuch as poetry, according to our understanding of the materialist conception of history, was part of the superstructure determined in the last instance by the economic basis of society. But in applying this theory to the literature of the past we were too ready to see in the economic basis only the relations of production through which one class exploited another, and to see in literature only their reflection. Caudwell, however, never forgot that the economic basis of society is not only the relations but also the forces of production, the economic activity of work. He thus gave a new meaning to the statement that poetry is an economic activity.

Contrasting human work with the activity of animals, Marx said in *Capital*:

> A spider conducts operations that resemble those of a weaver, and a bee puts to shame many an architect in the construction of her cells. But what distinguishes the worst architect from the best of bees is this, that the architect raises his structure in imagination before he erects it in reality.

The source of poetry, Caudwell says, is in this peculiarly human power. Man alone can direct his energy to the realization in the future of the aim he imagines now. Through poetry, through his harvest songs, he depicts what he wants to make real; and through the rhythms and images of poetry and its

182

heightening of collective emotion he arouses and directs his energy to the work of creation. Poetry is an economic activity in this sense: it is part of the work by which man makes himself human.

The importance of Caudwell's work, I said, was its relevance to class consciousness. In order to know who we, the working class, are, we must know that it is through work that man becomes human. To be aware that we are exploited is only the beginning of class consciousness. We are not only the exploited class. From the activity of work has come poetry, the power to heighten life by communicating in beauty the experience of being man. To be alive today is to possess the power to do the work of poetry by creating in the socialist revolution a world where man will be free to realize his humanity. Our class consciousness must be knowledge of that power and resolution to use it.

I also went regularly to the meetings of the Writers Group, which had now been revived. I gave a talk on Shaw, and I was urged to make it into a book.

Then one day when I was going along Old Compton Street I saw coming towards me, walking on the kerb like a boy unaware of his surroundings, my friend Arch – who in Ruhleben had said to me about my poetry 'You act'. I had not seen him since Switzerland, when, doing well as a journalist in Geneva, he had leased a furnished chalet by the lake and brought out his father and mother from England so that they might have some rest and pleasure before they died, and one of his sisters had come to look after them; I had gone down from Basle to spend a Christmas with them. He was now happily married to a woman who was an artist, and they had a son. He had just rented a manor house near Gillingham in Dorset, The Old House, which he was making into a country guest house, and he urged me to come down for a week-end.

I went in June, 1947. I remember as if it were yesterday standing with him on the lawn in the garden before twilight. The stone of the south-west front of the manor house was almost golden, and the only sounds were voices from a farm on the other side of a lane and a maze of swallows circling over a pond beside the manor stables. The peace seemed to enter into me, and in an access of longing I said, 'I wish I could live here.'

Some days after my return to London a letter came from Arch reminding me how one day in 1919, as we lay on the grass in Hyde Park and he picked at a fallen leaf, he had told me he was sometimes starving, and I had sold out £50 war loan for him. Now he wanted to repay it, he said, with the accumulated compound interest of twenty-eight years by partitioning off some of the attic in his manor house for me and giving me my food at what it cost the cook, and there I would be free to write.

Since Claire and I had separated, I had saved over £200 (the money left me by my mother had gone during times of unemployment). Encouraged by the praise given to my lectures on Caudwell and on Shaw, I decided I would go down to The Old House and write the book on Shaw, and the advance royalties on it and what should still be left of my savings would keep me while I wrote another book.

So in August, when the room in the attic was ready, I said goodbye at the Embassy, and went wearily – for I suddenly felt exhausted – with parcels of old letters and papers to the wartime salvage bin which still stood outside Notting Hill Gate station.

For some weeks I only went short walks, as if I were a convalescent, but in the autumn I began to explore the countryside, planning on an ordnance map where I would go, and coming back content after ten or fifteen miles along lanes and roads still almost empty of traffic, and over the great bare hills behind Mere, marked on the map with tumuli and prehistoric lychets, whose traces I could just make out.

I loved Dorset, beautiful and remote; and I had a sense I had not known before of the earth haunted by forgotten being. Sometimes it was like a presence, and once I wondered what would happen if I yielded myself. I tried; and the molten sun was shouting in the sky. 'Is that real, or am I acting?' I thought. If it was real, the whole earth was living. 'There is no thought without matter': when I read that sentence in Stalin's *Dialectical and Historical Materialism*, I thought of matter as lifeless and no less distinct from myself than the ink on the page, devoid of the meaning in the words which became part of my thinking. But supposing this moment were true, supposing it was this wonder of the sun which was the basis of thought?

'Where indeed would you land up if you thought that?' I said to myself.

The desk at which I worked was close beside a small window in the end wall of the house, from which the roof of a lower wing projected at right angles; and I looked along the green and yellow and russet tiles, against which the swallows used to come and rest their quivering bodies, to the ascending slope of a field, in which there was an oak mentioned in the Domesday Book, its vast gaping trunk held with bands of iron; and near a group of trees at the farther end of the field I could see on the skyline the spire of the village church. My eye often used to go to it in the long waits between the sentences. Shaw also, as he described in an early essay, cycling one day in the country and passing a village church, had dismounted and leaned his cycle against the wall, and gone in and felt that the place was holy. If what I was writing about him was true, he was wrong, and the spire I looked at was the unliving past. Yet it was as familiar as myself.

The thesis of my book was indicated by its title: *A Good Man Fallen Among Fabians.* Shaw as a young man hated 'the accursed middle-class institutions' which 'starved, thwarted, misled and corrupted' the members of that class. He read Marx's *Capital,* and realized that these middle-class institutions were based upon capitalist exploitation. 'From that hour,' he said, 'I became a man with some business in the world' – to hasten the coming of the inevitable and imminent revolution. In the last of his novels, *An Unsocial Socialist,* and in the *Unpleasant Plays* he exposed the loathsomeness of capitalist society: the landlords take their profit from the slums 'as flies fatten on filth'. Yet ten years later, when he chose as his subject a more significant form of capitalist exploitation than slum landlordism, namely the arms industry, he no longer spoke of exploitation and it was the capitalist, the armaments magnate himself, who was to make the revolution. This change, I said, was due to the influence of Fabianism. When faced in the 1880's with the choice of joining the Fabian Society or the Social Democratic Federation, which he described as respectively middle-class and proletarian, Shaw chose the Fabian Society; for the crushing of the Paris Commune and Bloody Sunday in Trafalgar Square was proof,

185

he said, that to expect socialism through revolution on the barricades was romanticism. This loss of faith in revolutionary action by the working class weakened his plays. Though the conviction never left him that bourgeois society would soon pass into history, and though his sense of this impending change and of its necessity was the source of his dramatic vision, he weakened the dramatic conflict by failure to show in the bourgeois world the power of the working class that would bring the change about.

There was truth in this thesis; but it became distorted through my not having faced my own conflict.

When Shaw had abandoned his first expectation that by the end of the nineteenth century the proletariat would have carried out the socialist revolution, he placed his hope of change in humanity. His ground for hope was his belief, expressed in the preface to the *Pleasant Plays,* that there was a revival of the spirit of the Middle Ages. The Middle Ages meant for Shaw a society where men were conscious that they were members one of another, and symbolized that membership in the cathedral. To this common humanity Shaw, in *The Perfect Wagnerite,* gave the name of 'Godhead'. Therefore in his dramatic criticism he said that the theatre, if it is true to itself, is 'a cathedral'; for the 'Godhead' of humanity is present in the unity, awakened by dramatic art, of audience, players and playwright. And since the theatre, he said, is also 'a factory of thought', the performance of the play is the clarification of what men must do to realize their 'Godhead'. The revival of the spirit of the Middle Ages meant that men were now casting off the self-centred individualism of the age of reason and of capitalism, and were becoming again conscious of the working within themselves of the power of their 'Godhead'.

I said in my book that since humanity is continuously changing, the religious hypostasization of humanity as 'Godhead' was idealism. Under the influence of this idealism Shaw looked to an armaments manufacturer inspired by a metaphysical 'will' to bring about socialism, not to the revolutionary action of the working class. Therefore when in 1917 the working class carried out the revolution, Shaw did not realize that a new era had begun in the history of humanity. For he wrote in the preface to *Saint Joan* :

186

I have before me the letter of a Catholic priest. 'In your play,' he writes, 'I see the dramatic presentation of the conflict of the Regal, sacerdotal and Prophetical powers, in which Joan was crushed. To me it is not the victory of any one of them over the others that will bring peace and the Reign of the Saints in the Kingdom of God, but their fruitful interaction in a costly but noble state of tension.' The Pope himself could not put it better; nor can I. We must accept the tension, and maintain it nobly without letting ourselves be tempted to relieve it by burning the thread.

I commented:

These words were written, by a man professing himself a communist, six years after the Socialist Revolution. That revolution had already burned the threads.

To make that comment, which implied that with the socialist revolution tension was over, I had to suppress the knowledge of tension in myself.

I was moved by Shaw's conception of a humanity of whose unity all individuals were part. Though I resisted the emotion, I felt myself part of this 'Godhead' as I did not feel myself part of the revolutionary movement I opposed to it. While I was working on *The Perfect Wagnerite* in which Shaw had expressed this conception of humanity, I went to see my father in Salisbury, where he was now living in a private hotel, my stepmother having died some months before the war. I had gone over several times to see him since I had come to The Old House, and we talked together in friendliness, sometimes about Christianity and communism. On this day, as I was going back to the station to get the train to Gillingham, I turned into the Cathedral Close. I went and sat on a wooden seat on the edge of the wide green sward, and looked across to the West Front and the soaring spire. I rose, and walked across the grass, and entered the building. After a few steps I stood still and looked towards the altar, and I thought that I also felt, like Shaw, that the place was holy.

Next day, as I was writing at my desk, there came back to my mind the sentence from Dostoevsky which I had kept secret:

187

The good that you mean to do, do not do it out of envy but for the sake of God. I am writing out of envy, I thought. Shaw had the courage of the life that was in him, and he had not been afraid, as I am afraid, to face what God meant for him. Therefore, unlike him, I cannot write in freedom, with that self speaking into my mind who in a cathedral wants to worship. So I revenge myself on him by misusing Marxism to prove myself superior.

I didn't follow the thought further for fear of strengthening my belief in God, yet knew that I should not let that fear stop me from facing the conflict between my profession of Marxism and my religious emotion.

I was similiarly held back by fear when late in 1947 the newly founded Cominform said that the world was now divided into two hostile camps, and at its Congress held early in 1948, the British Party changed its line. It said that the task of the Party now was no longer to ensure Labour's continuance in power but to 'unite the struggle of the working class in defence of its standard of living'. The Report which was to be submitted to Congress said:

> We need to recall how the British workers have always been willing to fight in defence of their interests. They did it on a grand scale against the Tory offensive after the end of the first World War. They showed their solidarity with the Soviet Union in the epic story of the 'Jolly George' in 1920, in their support of the miners in 1921 and 1926, in the great Hunger Marches, in their support for the Spanish Republic, in the great Unity Campaign in 1932-4; in the fight against Mosley and Hitler; in their solidarity with the colonial peoples. It is this record which is the pride of the movement.

I sent in a contribution to the pre-Congress discussion in the Party press, in which I said that it was a serious political error not even to mention in the list of the workers' struggles the part they had played in the war against fascism. The Party's task was not simply to 'unite the struggle of the working class in defence of its standard of living'; its task was to carry forward the unity achieved under working class leader-

188

ship in the war again fascism into the fight for the socialist revolution.

There was more on my mind than this. In the revolution, as Caudwell showed, man continued the advance from the animal to the human by winning freedom. The united struggle against fascism was the approach to this revolution, and it must not be obliterated by silence. To do so was to obscure the content of the class struggle, which was not merely that the workers should defend their living standard, but that they should lead the nation in the common advance of man. Which side were we on in the class struggle if we thus obscured its content?

But just as before the war I questioned my own motives in criticizing the Party's conception of unity rather than clearly face the possibility that it was not I who was wrong but the Party, so now I turned the question against myself. 'On which side am I in the class struggle,' I thought, 'when I thus criticize the Party for attaching too much weight to the workers' defence of their standard of living? I myself am living in a Dorset manor house, remote from the Party and from the daily struggle in which I once said the bourgeois intellectual must take active part if he wants to think as a Marxist. In this comfortable isolation I am becoming in Lenin's phrase, "a godseeker". I act the mystic and pretend to myself that I can hear the sun in the sky. When I say that the workers must lead the nation "in the common advance of man", is that not rhetoric, and is the emotion by which I want to be stirred essentially different from my religious response to Shaw's "humanity"?'

I could not answer, and went on with my book. I finished it in 1949, and it was published in the following year; it was praised in the Party press, but otherwise aroused little notice. I was now back in London, for the Dorset guest house had proved a failure and Arch had had to give it up. I was teaching again at the Soviet Embassy, and was once more active in my local Branch.

In 1951 *The British Road to Socialism* was published. The nation, we now said, must carry on the fight against imperialism, and it was in the consciousness of their membership of the nation that the working class must lead the fight.

As part of the campaign for the new policy, conferences were organized on the defence of the British cultural tradition, and

I was asked in 1953 to take a week-end school on the theme 'Culture is a weapon in the fight for socialism'. Thinking out what I would say, I felt that the theme stated no more than a half truth. At the school I said that culture, as Caudwell had written of poetry in *Illusion and Reality,* heightens our consciousness of the world we want to win and our energy to win it. In this sense it was true that culture is a weapon in the fight for socialism. But the truth depended on recognition of the greater truth that socialism is a weapon in the fight for culture. For our final aim was not the establishment of a political and economic structure, but the heightening of human life. Without this recognition, the slogan became a perversion of the truth, since it degraded culture into a means to a political end.

It seemed to me that the political end itself was thereby perverted, and that this was the weakness of *The British Road to Socialism.* For the freedom to be won through socialism was the freedom of humanity, and neither this freedom nor the road to it could be conceived in national terms. At a meeting of the Cultural Committee, of which I was a member, I said that since the enrichment of human culture was our final aim, the Cultural Committee should have equal standing with the Political Committee in the leadership of the Party. The proposal met with no response, and I said no more.

I continued to take part in local activity. One evening after a Branch meeting we were to distribute leaflets in a municipal election campaign, since there were Party members standing. I went with my bundle to a tall block of flats near King's Cross. I took the lift to the top floor, where from a window at the end of a passage I could see the wide darkness and the lights of London like a flat sky of stars, and then I started down the dim concrete stairs. I folded and stuck the leaflets, announcing a meeting against the high rents of the flats, through the letterboxes, wondering whether my care not to let the flap fall back noisily was because I didn't want to disturb the people within or because I would rather not be seen. There was nobody on the staircase, but as I was at the head of the next flight down, I heard from the landing I had already done the sound of a door gently opening. I looked round, and in the narrow crack of the open door stood a young child, her left shoulder turned towards me. We looked at each other in silence. Then as I went

190

on down the empty stairs, I heard the door close. I was most deeply moved, beyond all thought. I said to myself that I would not have experienced this moment without Party membership, and that there was an obligation upon me to find out and say what it meant. I did not know why I should have been so moved; nor when I began to describe the memory did I know why it had returned to me. Only now, in the moment of writing, have I remembered the closing of the door after Sonja's last words: 'You have not had the strength to do what you ought to have done'.

Whether or not I then decided, without knowing, to write such a book as this, I cannot tell. But I remember that I now recalled what my father had said to me years before: 'A man must speak out the truth that is in him'.

The conscious decision was made some time after the Twentieth Congress of the Communist Party of the Soviet Union. I was shocked by Khrushchev's revelations which confirmed as truth what I had rejected as propaganda. Still more disturbing was the absence of any serious attempt to find out how these errors and crimes came to be committed, and Palme Dutt's dismissal of them in the *Labour Monthly* as mere spots on the Soviet sun.

Then came the rising in Hungary. Whether its suppression by the Soviet Union was necessary or not – and I came to the conclusion that it was – the rising itself was against the same inhuman tyranny as that which Khrushchev had exposed. Again there was the question: how could the socialist revolution have been thus perverted? To say that the perversion had been caused by 'Stalinism' was not an answer. It was not the work of one man, nor was it the result of the 'cult of the individual'. There had been no cult of the individual. Individuals had been imprisoned without trial and put to death. If the socialist revolution, as I had believed in it, was not being realized, it was certain that the causes were not to be found in the Soviet Union alone. The formal fact of the Communist International having been dissolved during the war had not changed the essential fact that communism was a world movement. It was not the activity of a party in one country only, but of the parties in all countries. Therefore our Party in Britain also bore responsibility, and so did its individual members, since the

191

Party only had its being through them. When I heard on the wireless the last broadcast from Budapest radio station, the appeal for help, and then silence, I had asked myself whether I could stay in the Party; but to resign seemed now too easy an escape from a responsibility I shared.

It was around this time that the conscious decision was made to write this book. I felt, rather than knew, that my responsibility was that I had failed through silence. I would now break it, and by describing how I came to join the Party I would try to show the intellectual and moral necessity for an individual to make himself a communist.

I began the book in 1957. I thought at first that I would call it 'Becoming a Communist', and later that I would have to add a question-mark. Since finishing it, I have asked myself whether I have not done the opposite of what I intended. I can imagine a reader saying 'You have shown the truth, not of communism, but of what you denied in the name of communism'.

There is reason, I think, for such criticism. The book goes contrary to communism in its self-centredness and in its withdrawal from the life around me. I have described how an individual, whose presence in the world I took for granted because he was myself, came to join a Communist Party which was likewise there for him to join. Since I thus assumed their existence, I related neither self nor Party to the movement of which they were part.

I failed to do so because I thought it would be presumptuous to reason from myself to the Party. In reality, it was still more presumptuous to imagine that I was exceptional, and that other people, and the political organizations which act only through them, were immune from my own conflicts. I believe now that there were grounds for my doubts about the policy of the Party in relation to unity against fascism and about its understanding of the content of the socialist revolution. I was wrong to turn my questions against myself. I did so because this required less intellectual and moral strength than to face my responsibility as human being for the policy of the Party of which I remain a member.

For I still believe that communism is necessary to the freedom of mankind.

I wish to close with a memory.

One evening in the winter of 1948 my father had a fall in his room and fractured his thigh. He got up and walked downstairs.

After a night of pain he was taken to Salisbury Infirmary, where Constance, Cecil and I visited him. The last time I saw him, he had been settled for the night and was lying on his back, with the bedclothes tucked up to his great chin, on which there was a fine white stubble. I peeled an orange for him, and as he opened his mouth wide for the next segment, in his eyes a light dancing, I said to him, 'You are like a great cuckoo'. When I went away, I kissed him on the forehead, and wanted to say to him, but didn't, 'No man can have had a better father'.

The next day he died.

GEORGE ALLEN & UNWIN LTD

Head Office
40 Museum Street, London, W.C.1
Telephone: 01-405 8577

Sales, Distribution and Accounts Departments
Park Lane, Hemel Hempstead, Herts.
Telephone: 0442 2361/2

Athens: 34 Panepistimiou Street
Auckland: P.O. Box 36013, Northcote Central N.4
Barbados: P.O. Box 222, Bridgetown
Bombay: 103/5 Fort Street, Bombay 1
Buenos Aires: Escritorio 454-459, Florida 165
Beirut: Deeb Building, Jeanne d'Arc Street
Calcutta: 285J Bepin Behari Ganguli Street, Calcutta 12
Cape Town: 68 Shortmarket Street
Hong Kong: 105 Wing On Mansion, 26 Hancow Road, Kowloon
Ibadan: P.O. Box 62
Karachi: Karachi Chambers, McLeod Road
Madras: 2/18 Mount Road, Madras
Mexico: Villalongin 32, Mexico 5, D.F.
Nairobi: P.O. Box 30583
New Delhi: 13-14 Asaf Ali Road, New Delhi 1
Philippines: P.O. Box 157, Quezon City D-502
Rio de Janeiro: Caixa Postal 2537-Zc-00
Singapore: 36c Prinsep Street, Singapore 7
Sydney N.S.W.: Bradbury House, 55 York Street
Tokyo: P.O. Box 1728, Tokyo 100-91
Toronto: 81 Curlew Drive, Don Mills

M. PHILIPS PRICE
My Three Revolutions

Mr Philips Price, who was for over twenty-six years a member of the House of Commons, and was earlier a foreign correspondent for the old *Manchester Guardian* and *Daily Herald*, can truly claim to have lived through three revolutions. He can therefore write of them at first hand. First he was in Russia when the 1917 revolution took place; here a complete social upheaval occurred in line with the history and tradition of the country. Later he was in Germany and saw the early phase of the revolution that swept away the Hohenzollern régime. Finally, as an active politician he watched at close quarters the changes, some slow and some swift, that transferred the Britain of the Empire into the Britain of the welfare state, a revolution that is by no means complete, for the economic problems that have resulted have still to be resolved.

On an autobiographical base, Mr Philips Price records the events of a long life often in close touch with world-shaking events and his observations of over eighty years of changing society.

SIR ROBERT TREDGOLD
The Rhodesia that was My Life

'With his particular record and background, Sir Robert's views carry special weight.' *Contemporary Review.*

'Sir Robert emerges as a man of liberal sentiment, strong character, firm beliefs, a ready wit, and great humility and understanding. All who are interested in Rhodesia will find this a nostalgic and yet refreshing book.' *Race.*

LONDON: GEORGE ALLEN AND UNWIN LTD